PEARSON

COMMON CORE

Literature

Student Companion
All-in-One Workbook

GRADE 6

PEARSON

HOBOKEN, NEW JERSEY • BOSTON, MASSACHUSETTS
CHANDLER, ARIZONA • GLENVIEW, ILLINOIS

ISBN-13: 978-0-13-327114-0
ISBN-10:   0-13-327114-5
10 V001 18 17 16 15

CONTENTS

Comparing Texts: "Lob's Girl" by Joan Aiken and "Jeremiah's Song" by Walter Dean Myers

UNIT 1 • PART 3 Developing Insights

"The King of Mazy May" by Jack London

"To Klondike We've Paid Our Fare" by H. J. Dunham

"Gold Rush: The Journey by Land"

"A Woman's View of the Gold Rush" by Mary Ballou

"Chinese and African Americans in the Gold Rush" by Johns Hopkins University

"Birds Struggle to Recover from Egg Thefts of 1800s" by Edie Lau

UNIT 2 • PART 1 Setting Expectations

UNIT 2 • PART 2 Guided Exploration

"The Drive-In Movies" by Gary Soto

"Names/Nombres" by Julia Alvarez

"Langston Terrace" by Eloise Greenfield

Name _____ Date _____

Unit 1: Short Stories
Big Question Vocabulary—1

The Big Question: Is conflict always bad?

It is impossible to have relationships with people without some conflict arising. One kind of conflict is an argument between friends. The following words are used to talk about arguments.

argue: to disagree with someone in words, often in an angry way

conclude: to bring something to an end

convince: to get another person to think the same way as you

issue: a problem or subject that people discuss

resolve: to find an acceptable way to deal with a problem or difficulty

DIRECTIONS: *Write about a disagreement that you have had with a friend or family member, using the words in parentheses.*

1. **Description of the disagreement:**

(argue, issue)

2. **How did each party to the disagreement try to get the other person to change his or her thinking?**

(convince)

3. **What was the end result?**

(resolve, conclude)

Unit 1: Short Stories
Big Question Vocabulary—2

The Big Question: Is conflict always bad?

One kind of conflict is a game or sport, which is played according to rules. Most people agree that games or sports are "good" conflict.

challenge: *n.* something that tests a person's strength, skill, or ability; *v.* to question whether something is fair or right

compete: to try to gain something, or to be better or more successful at something than someone else

game: an activity or a sport in which people play against one another according to agreed rules

lose: to not be best or first at something

win: to be best or first at something

DIRECTIONS: *Using the words in parentheses, describe a game or sport that you are familiar with.*

1. How do you play?

(game, challenge)

2. Who plays?

(compete)

3. What is the end result?

(win, lose)

Unit 1: Short Stories
Big Question Vocabulary—3

The Big Question: Is conflict always bad?

Sometimes conflict can lead to violent battles or wars between opposing groups. The following words can help you talk about these kinds of conflict.

battle: encounter in which opposing groups compete, fight, or argue to try to win

defend: to act in support of someone's being hurt or criticized

negotiate: to discuss something to reach an agreement

resist: to stop yourself from doing something you would very much like to do

survival: the state of continuing to exist when there is a risk that you might die

DIRECTIONS: *Answer the questions below using the words in parentheses in the boxes.*

When the early settlers came to America, the Native Americans were already living here.

1. What were two ways the settlers could have dealt with the problem of sharing land with the Native Americans?

2. What are possible results of each decision?

1.

(negotiate)

(battle)

2.

(survival)

(defend)

Name _____ Date _____

Unit 1: Short Stories
Applying the Big Question

 Is conflict always bad?

DIRECTIONS: *Complete the chart below to apply what you have learned about the "pros and cons" of conflict. One row has been completed for you.*

Example	Type of Conflict	How the conflict is resolved	What is bad about the conflict	What is good about the conflict	What I learned
From Literature	In "The Circuit," a boy wants to stay in one place, but his family must often move.	Panchito must accept the hardships of his family's life.	Panchito feels uncomfortable in school; he has to leave a new friend.	Panchito sees how others live; he learns something new with each new experience.	Some conflicts cannot be resolved; conflicts can be a source of courage.
From Literature					
From Science					
From Social Studies					
From Real Life					

Name _____ Date _____

"Stray" by Cynthia Rylant
Writing About the Big Question

Is conflict always bad?

Big Question Vocabulary

argue	battle	challenge	compete	conclude
convince	defend	game	issue	lose
negotiate	resist	resolve	survival	win

A. *Use one or more words from the list above to complete each sentence.*

1. Through research, scientists were able to _____ that people with pets are happier.

2. In addition to making people happy, a pet dog can _____ a family home against intruders.

3. In spite of the evidence in favor of pets, some people still _____ the urge to adopt pets.

4. Many parents feel that taking care of a pet is too great a _____, especially for younger children.

B. *Respond to each item with a complete sentence.*

1. Describe a pet that you have had or would like to have.

   _____

   _____

2. Explain how the pet you described helped or would help you. Use at least two Big Question vocabulary words.

   _____

   _____

C. *In "Stray," Doris's parents tell her they cannot afford to keep the stray dog she found. Complete the sentence below. Then, write a short paragraph connecting this situation to the Big Question.*

   Owning a pet can sometimes cause difficulties because _____

   _____

   _____

   _____

   _____

"Stray" by Cynthia Rylant
Reading: Use Prior Knowledge to Make Predictions

A **prediction** is a logical guess about what will happen next in a story. You can **use your prior knowledge** to help you make predictions. To do this, relate what you already know to the details in a story. For example, you have prior knowledge about stray animals. If you haven't seen one, you have read about them. You know how they look. You know how they make you feel. Then, as you read details about the abandoned puppy in "Stray," you are ready to make a **prediction,** a logical guess, about what might happen next.

What if your prediction turns out to be wrong? No problem. Part of the fun of reading is adjusting your predictions as you get more details. As you read, use story clues and your own knowledge to make predictions along the way.

DIRECTIONS: *You have prior knowledge about dogs. You know a lot about how children relate to adults in a family. You have prior knowledge about the costs of owning a pet. Start with your prior knowledge. Combine it with a detail from the story. Then, make a prediction on the chart that follows. One entry has been modeled for you.*

Prior Knowledge	Detail From Story	Prediction
About strays They're hungry. +	This one shivers with cold. =	Doris will bring it in and feed it.
1. About dogs _____ + _____	_____ = _____	_____ _____
2. About children and adults in a family _____ + _____	_____ = _____	_____ _____
3. About the costs of owning a pet _____ + _____	_____ = _____	_____ _____

"Stray" by Cynthia Rylant
Literary Analysis: Plot

The **plot** of "Stray" is the arrangement of events in the story. The elements of plot include:

- **Exposition:** introduction of the setting, characters, and basic situation
- **Conflict:** the story's central problem
- **Rising action:** events that increase the tension
- **Climax:** high point of the story when the story's outcome becomes clear
- **Falling action:** events that follow the climax
- **Resolution:** the final outcome

All the events in a plot follow one after another in a logical way. Like most stories, "Stray" centers on a conflict or struggle. You keep reading because you want to find out who will win the conflict or how the problem will be solved. At the climax of the story, you know who wins. The problem is solved. The story ends.

A. DIRECTIONS: *The following questions focus on the exposition, the rising action, and the falling action in "Stray." Answer each question in the space provided.*

1. The exposition introduces the setting, characters, and basic situation. Here is one exposition detail:

    Exposition detail: Snow has fallen.

    What is another exposition detail?

    Exposition detail: _____

    _____

2. The events in the rising action come before the climax. There are many events in the rising action of "Stray." Here is one event in the rising action:

    Rising action event: Doris meets the dog.

    On the following lines, write two additional events that happen in the rising action.

    Rising action events:

    a. _____

    _____

    b. _____

    _____

3. In "Stray," the story winds up quickly after the climax. Here is one event in the falling action:

    Falling action event: Mr. Lacey tells Doris he took the dog to the pound.

    What is another event that happens in the falling action?

    Falling action event: _____

    _____

"**Stray**" by Cynthia Rylant
Vocabulary Builder

Word List

exhausted   grudgingly   ignore   starvation   timidly   trudged

A. DIRECTIONS: *In each question below, think about the meaning of the underlined word from the Word List. Then, answer the questions.*

1. If a puppy enters a room <u>timidly</u>, is he running or moving cautiously? Why?

   Answer: _____

   Explanation: _____

2. If you admire someone, will you help that person <u>grudgingly</u> or willingly? Explain.

   Answer: _____

   Explanation: _____

3. If a team chooses to <u>ignore</u> its coach, might the coach be pleased or angry? Why?

   Answer: _____

   Explanation: _____

4. If someone <u>trudged</u> through the woods, would she move quickly? Why or why not?

   Answer: _____

   Explanation: _____

5. If you are <u>exhausted</u>, what might you do? Why?

   Answer: _____

   Explanation: _____

6. If a bear eats too much, would it face <u>starvation</u>? Why or why not?

   Answer: _____

   Explanation: _____

B. Word Study: *The Latin suffix -ation changes a verb to a noun. It means "the condition of being ___ed (past tense verb)." Change each underlined verb into a noun by adding -ation. Answer the question using the new word.*

1. How might a mother and her child feel if they were to <u>separate</u> in a crowd?

   _____

2. What do you like to <u>converse</u> about?

   _____

3. What things do you <u>admire</u> in a person?

   _____

Name _____ Date _____

"Stray" by Cynthia Rylant

Conventions: Common, Proper, and Possessive Nouns

Common and Proper Nouns; Possessives

Nouns may be either common or proper. Some nouns are made up of more than one word.

- A **common noun** names any one of a group of people, places, things, or ideas.
  Examples: girl, city, dogs, chairs, freedom, computer room, teacher, ice cream

- A **proper noun** names a particular person, place, or thing. A proper noun always begins with a capital letter. *Do not confuse a proper noun with a common noun that is capitalized because it is the first word of a sentence.*
  Examples: Doris, Mr. Amos Lacey, North Carolina, "The Homecoming," Asian American Museum, United States of America

The **possessive** of a noun shows ownership or possession. An **apostrophe,** which looks like a comma that has jumped up into the space above the line, is used to form the possessive.

- To form the possessive of a singular noun (naming one person, place, thing, or idea), add an apostrophe and an **s.**
  Examples: Doris's dog, West Virginia's farmland, the computer room's radiator

- To form the possessive of a plural noun that ends in **s,** add only the apostrophe.
  Examples: five minutes' time, the Beckmans' address, the girls' team

- To form the possessive of a plural noun that does *not* end in **s,** add an apostrophe and an **s.**
  Examples: children's stories, mice's cheese, the women's meeting

Never use an apostrophe to form the plural of a noun. Remember: An apostrophe, when used with a noun, shows ownership.

Incorrect: The birds' left their eggs behind in the nest.

Correct: The birds' eggs were left behind in their nest.

A. DIRECTIONS: *Underline each noun in the sentences below. Above each noun, write C if it is a common noun and P if it is a proper noun. Add another line under the possessive nouns.*

1. Cynthia Rylant discovered that her life's story interested children.

2. Rylant spent part of her childhood in West Virginia's hills.

3. Like the main character in "Stray," Rylant loves animals.

4. Doris wanted to keep the dog, but Mrs. Lacey objected.

5. Doris hoped she could overcome her parents' objections to the dog.

Name _____ Date _____

"**Stray**" by Cynthia Rylant
Support for Writing to Sources: Explanatory Text

Use the chart below to gather details about why Doris should be allowed to keep the puppy.

Details about the dog:
Details about Doris:
Details about the family:
Conclusion:

Now, use the details you have collected to write the list of reasons to keep the puppy. Be sure to use formal language, and write in complete sentences.

Name _____ Date _____

"Stray" by Cynthia Rylant
Support for Research and Technology: Brochure

Owning a pet can be very rewarding, but it can also be a lot of work. It is important to know how to properly care for an animal. Use the chart below to collect information you find on the Internet and from library resources. You will use the information to put together a brochure for new pet owners.

	Notes	Source
General feeding instructions		
Early training tips		
Keeping dogs happy and healthy		

Now, use your notes to draft your brochure. If possible, use a computer to write and design your brochure. Include pictures if available.

Name _____ Date _____

"The Tail" by Joyce Hansen

Writing About the Big Question

 Is conflict always bad?

Big Question Vocabulary

argue	battle	challenge	compete	conclude
convince	defend	game	issue	lose
negotiate	resist	resolve	survival	win

A. *Use one or more words from the list above to complete each sentence.*

1. One way to entertain a child is to play a _____ with him or her.

2. Parents and children are likely to _____ with each other.

3. It often seems important to both sides to _____ an argument.

4. Sometimes it is possible to _____ an outcome that makes everyone happy.

B. *Respond to each item with a complete sentence.*

1. Describe two arguments you have had with someone in your family.

   _____

   _____

2. Explain how you managed to negotiate an agreement in one of the arguments you had. Use at least two of the Big Question vocabulary words.

   _____

   _____

C. *Complete this sentence. Then, write a brief paragraph in which you connect this sentence to the Big Question.*

Conflicts between children and their parents can have positive outcomes when

_____

_____

_____

_____

_____

_____

"The Tail" by Joyce Hansen
Reading: Use Details to Make Inferences

When you **make inferences,** you make logical assumptions about something that is not directly stated in the text. To make inferences, use the **details** that the author provides.

Details in the text + What you know = Inference

Look at the details, shown in italics, in the following sentence.
Arnie *ran* to the mailbox *as fast as he could* to see if Jim's letter had *finally* arrived.

You can make two inferences from the details and from what you know.

- From *finally,* you can infer that Arnie has been waiting to hear from Jim.
- Because Arnie runs fast, you can infer that he is eager to get the letter.

DIRECTIONS: *As you read "The Tail," find details that help you make three inferences. Write two details and your logical inference in each row of boxes below.*

A.

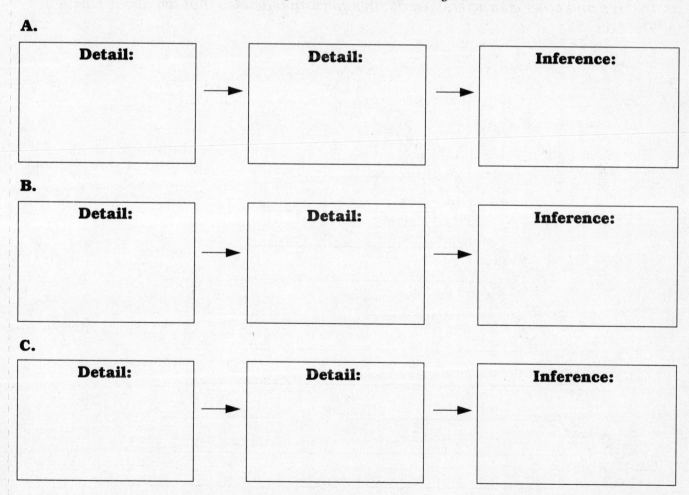

| Detail: | Detail: | Inference: |

B.

| Detail: | Detail: | Inference: |

C.

| Detail: | Detail: | Inference: |

Name _____ Date _____

"The Tail" by Joyce Hansen
Literary Analysis: Characterization

Characterization is the way writers develop and reveal information about characters.

- **Direct characterization:** a writer makes direct statements about a character.
- **Indirect characterization:** a writer suggests information through a character's thoughts, words, and actions as well as what other characters say and think about the character.

In this passage from "The Tail," the writer uses Tasha's thoughts to give an indirect characterization of Junior: He is cute but very troublesome.

> Junior held her hand and stared up at her with an innocent look in his bright brown eyes, which everyone thought were so cute. Dimples decorated his round cheeks as he smiled and nodded at me every time Ma gave me an order. I knew he was just waiting for her to leave so he could torment me.

DIRECTIONS: *In each part of the pyramid below, jot down direct statements as well as Tasha's and other characters' words, thoughts, and actions that tell about Tasha in "The Tail."*

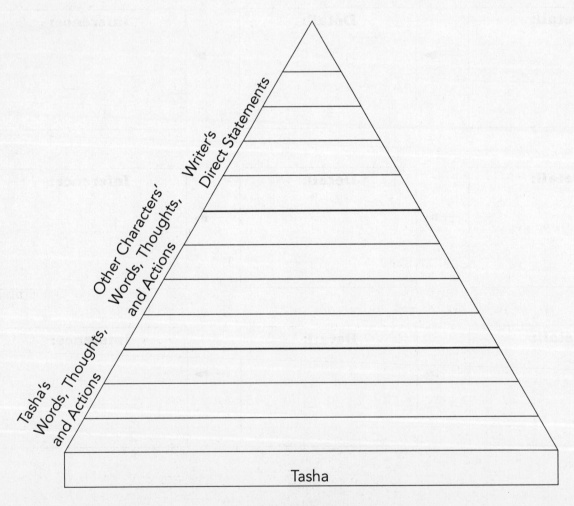

Name _____ Date _____

"The Tail" by Joyce Hansen
Vocabulary Builder

Word List

anxious   gnawing   mauled   routine   spasm   vow

A. DIRECTIONS: Synonyms *are words that are similar in meaning. Find and write a synonym for each vocabulary word. Then, use each synonym in a sentence that makes the meaning of the word clear. The first one has been done for you.*

1. *gnawing*

   Synonym: <u>chewing</u>

   Sentence: Rodents have been chewing on the bark of this tree.

2. *mauled*

   Synonym: _____

   Sentence: _____

3. *spasm*

   Synonym: _____

   Sentence: _____

4. *anxious*

   Synonym: _____

   Sentence: _____

5. *routine*

   Synonym: _____

   Sentence: _____

6. *vow*

   Synonym: _____

   Sentence: _____

B. WORD STUDY: *Adding the Latin prefix* dis- *to a word often gives the word its opposite meaning. Think about the meaning of* dis- *in each underlined word. On the line before each sentence, write* T *if the statement is true and* F *if the statement is false. Then, explain your answer.*

1. _____ A person who is in <u>discomfort</u> does not feel well.

   _____

2. _____ If you are looking for something, you want it to <u>disappear.</u>

   _____

3. _____ To <u>disconnect</u> the television, you should plug it in.

   _____

"The Tail" by Joyce Hansen
Conventions: Personal and Possessive Pronouns

Personal pronouns refer to specific nouns or other pronouns that are named elsewhere in the text. **Possessive pronouns** show ownership. They can modify nouns or be used by themselves. Notice that a possessive pronoun never uses an apostrophe (').

PERSONAL PRONOUNS		POSSESSIVE PRONOUNS	
Singular	**Plural**	**Used Before Nouns**	**Used by Themselves**
I, me	we, us	my, our	mine, ours
you	you	your	yours
he, him, she, her, it	they, them	his, her, its, their	theirs

A. PRACTICE: *Underline every possessive or personal pronoun in each sentence.*

1. This is a photo of our family.
2. His gray hair is not too thick or too long, but it is just right.
3. Mother liked to carry her little kitten on her shoulder.
4. It troubles me that so few people really know my Papa as well as I do.

B. WRITING APPLICATION: *Rewrite each sentence to replace the noun with a possessive pronoun. Then, rewrite the sentence again to use a possessive pronoun by itself. The first one has been done for you.*

1. This backpack belongs to you.   This is your backpack.   The backpack is yours.
2. Kathy has a home on Grant Street.

_____

_____

3. The speech that I will make will be brief.

_____

_____

4. The cheers you heard came from us.

_____

_____

All-in-One Workbook
16

"The Tail" by Joyce Hansen
Support for Writing to Sources: Letter of Recommendation

DIRECTIONS: *If Tasha were to apply for a steady baby-sitting job, she would need a letter of recommendation. Use this chart to help you write a letter of recommendation for Tasha. On the chart, list her character traits, abilities, and experience.*

Character Traits	Abilities	Experience

Now, use the information from your chart to write a letter of recommendation.

"The Tail" by Joyce Hansen

Support for Research and Technology: Compare and Contrast

Fill out a Venn diagram for two outdoor children's games. Label each oval with the name of one game. In the part where the ovals overlap, write details that the games share. In the parts of the ovals that do not overlap, write details that are different for each game.

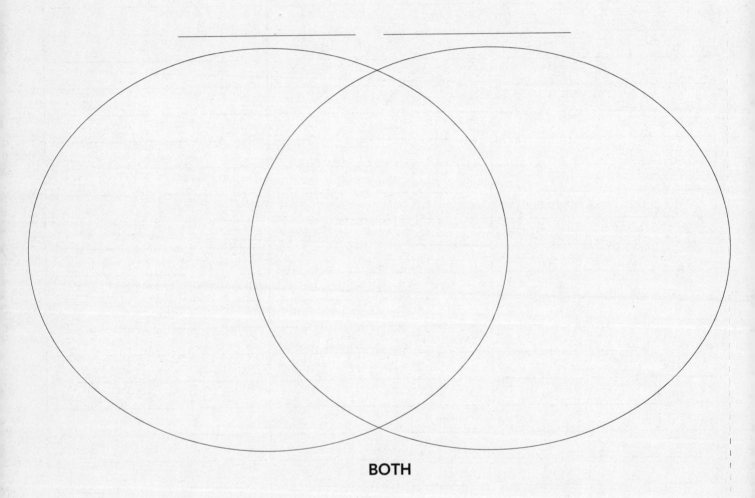

BOTH

Now, write a summary of the similarities and differences between the two games.

Name _____ Date _____

"Zlateh the Goat" by Isaac Bashevis Singer
Writing About the Big Question

Is conflict always bad?

Big Question Vocabulary

argue	battle	challenge	compete	conclude
convince	defend	game	issue	lose
negotiate	resist	resolve	survival	win

A. *Use one or more words from the list above to complete each sentence.*

1. Many people _____ homes and belongings in natural disasters.

2. The forces of nature can make _____ difficult.

3. Blizzards, hurricanes, wildfires, and floods can _____ even the strongest person.

4. To _____ nature, you have to be both strong and determined.

B. *Respond to each item with a complete sentence.*

1. What is the worst weather situation you have ever faced? Describe it.

_____

_____

2. Use at least two Big Question vocabulary words to tell how the forces of nature challenged you and how you reacted.

_____

_____

C. *Complete this sentence. Then, write a brief paragraph in which you connect this idea to the Big Question.*

One positive outcome of hardship or conflict can be _____

_____

_____

_____

_____

_____

_____

Name _____ Date _____

Reading: Use Prior Knowledge to Make Inferences

An **inference** is a logical assumption about information that is not directly stated. An inference is based on information you are given and your own thoughts. To make an inference, combine clues from the text with your own **prior knowledge,** or what you already know.

Clues in the text + What you know = Inference

Read this passage from "Zlateh the Goat."

> For Reuven the furrier it was a bad year, and after long hesitation he decided to sell Zlateh the goat.

- The passage tells you that Reuven hesitates before making his decision.
- Your prior knowledge tells you that people might hesitate before making difficult decisions.
- You can infer that Reuven's decision to sell the goat was not an easy decision for him to make.

DIRECTIONS: *The chart below lists story details from "Zlateh the Goat" and prior knowledge that you can use to make inferences. In the third box in each row, use the detail and the prior knowledge to make and write an inference.*

1.

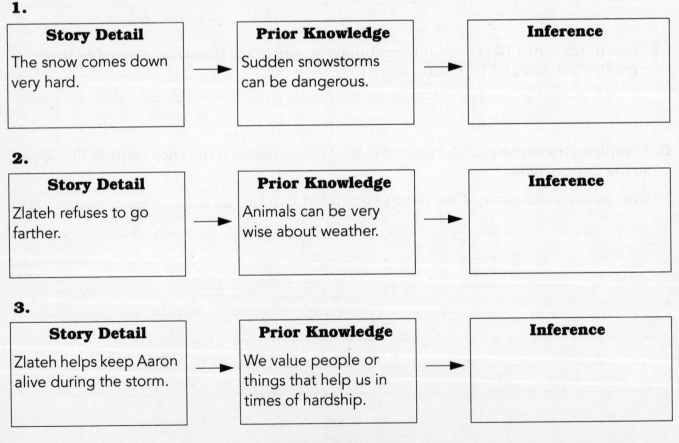

Story Detail	Prior Knowledge	Inference
The snow comes down very hard.	Sudden snowstorms can be dangerous.	

2.

Story Detail	Prior Knowledge	Inference
Zlateh refuses to go farther.	Animals can be very wise about weather.	

3.

Story Detail	Prior Knowledge	Inference
Zlateh helps keep Aaron alive during the storm.	We value people or things that help us in times of hardship.	

Name _____ Date _____

"Zlateh the Goat" by Isaac Bashevis Singer
Literary Analysis: Conflict and Resolution

A **conflict** is a struggle between opposing forces. In a short story, the conflict, or struggle, drives the action. Events contribute to the conflict or to the **resolution.** The resolution is the way in which the conflict is settled. Conflicts can be *external* or *internal*.

- **External conflict:** a character struggles against an outside force, such as another person or an element of nature. An example of external conflict is a fire that threatens the safety of a family and their home.
- **Internal conflict:** a character struggles within himself or herself to make a choice, take an action, or overcome a feeling. An example of internal conflict is a girl's desire to go skating with her friends when she knows she should stay home to do her homework.

A. DIRECTIONS: *Read the following sentences. On the lines, write* internal *or* external *to describe the conflict. Then, explain the opposing forces that cause the conflict.*

1. The peasants complained that because of the dry weather there would be a poor harvest of winter grain.

   Type of conflict: _____

   Forces in the conflict: _____

   _____

2. Aaron understood what taking the goat to Feivel meant, but he had to obey his father.

   Type of conflict: _____

   Forces in the conflict: _____

   _____

B. DIRECTIONS: *Review "Zlateh the Goat" to help you explain the resolution of each conflict in Exercise A.*

1. _____

   _____

2. _____

   _____

Name _____ Date _____

"**Zlateh the Goat**" by Isaac Bashevis Singer
Vocabulary Builder

Word List
astray   bound   exuded   flickering   splendor   trace

A. DIRECTIONS: *On the line before each sentence, write* T *if the statement is true or* F *if the statement is false. Then, explain your answer. The first one has been done for you.*

1. __F__ Aaron *bound* the snow to his jacket.
   Bound means "to tie," and Aaron cannot tie snow to his jacket.

2. _____ Someone who *exuded* a sense of despair would soon be happy.
   _____
   _____

3. _____ A sheep that has gone *astray* is with the other sheep.
   _____
   _____

4. _____ Most civilizations leave a *trace* of their existence behind.
   _____
   _____

5. _____ People in a family are often *bound* by affection and shared values.
   _____
   _____

6. _____ A candle flame would be *flickering* in a breeze.
   _____
   _____

7. _____ A person might be awed by the *splendor* of a huge palace.
   _____
   _____

B. WORD STUDY: *The Latin prefix* ex- *means "out," "from," or "beyond." Think about the meaning of the prefix* ex- *in each underlined word. Then, write an answer to each question.*

1. When might you <u>explain</u> an idea?
   _____

2. What kind of animal has an <u>external</u> shell?
   _____

3. What kind of sports are called <u>extreme</u> sports?
   _____

"Zlateh the Goat" by Isaac Bashevis Singer

Conventions: Interrogative, Indefinite, Reflexive, and Intensive Pronouns

Interrogative and Indefinite Pronouns

A **pronoun** is a word that takes the place of a noun or another pronoun.

- **Interrogative pronouns** are used in questions. Interrogative pronouns include *who, whom, whose, what,* and *which.*

- **Indefinite pronouns** refer to one or more unspecified people or objects. Indefinite pronouns include *some, one, other,* and *none.*

Reflexive and Intensive Pronouns

- **Reflexive pronouns** point to a person or thing receiving the action when that person or thing is the same as the one performing the action. *(I gave myself a pep talk. Jenna considers herself athletic.)*

- **Intensive Pronouns** add emphasis to another noun or pronoun. They are not essential to the meaning of the sentence. *(The judge herself heard the evidence. The team themselves chose the uniforms.)*

A. PRACTICE: *In each of these sentences, underline the interrogative, indefinite, reflexive, and intensive pronouns. Above the interrogative pronouns, write* Inter; *above the indefinite pronouns, write* Indef; *above the reflexive pronouns write* Refl; *and above the intensive pronouns, write* Intensv.

1. Who thought to name the goat *Zlateh?*

2. No one in Aaron's family wanted the goat to be sold.

3. Father himself was sad about selling the goat.

4. If Aaron could not find shelter for himself and Zlateh, they could die.

5. They sheltered themselves in a haystack.

6. All of Aaron's family welcomed him home with joy.

B. WRITING APPLICATION: *Write a brief paragraph about "Zlateh the Goat." Use at least three of the four types of pronouns in your paragraph. Then underline those pronouns.*

_____

_____

_____

_____

_____

Name _____ Date _____

Support for Writing to Sources: Persuasive Speech

Pretend that you are Aaron, and you want to persuade your father to keep Zlateh. Then, in the chart below, list at least two reasons to keep the goat. Use details from the story to support the reasons. List counterarguments Aaron's father might make. Then summarize your conclusion on the lines provided.

Reasons	Details That Support the Reason	Counterarguments

Conclusion:

_____

_____

Now, use the reasons you have written to write your persuasive speech.

Name _____ Date _____

"Zlateh the Goat" by Isaac Bashevis Singer

Support for Research and Technology: Comparison-and-Contrast Chart

To prepare to make a comparison-and-contrast chart about your hometown and a Jewish village in Eastern Europe before World War II, write the answers to these questions. Use online databases in your research.

1. What is the population of my hometown?

   _____

   _____

   What was the population of a typical Jewish village of the time?

   _____

   _____

2. What kinds of resources (libraries, schools, stores, churches, etc.) can be found in my hometown?

   _____

   _____

   What resources were available in a typical Jewish village of the time?

   _____

   _____

3. What things make up my way of life in my hometown? (For example, where do we shop for food or clothing? What do we do for entertainment? What kind of transportation and communication do we use?)

   _____

   _____

   _____

   What things characteristically made up the way of life in a typical Jewish village of the time?

   _____

   _____

   _____

"The Circuit" by Francisco Jiménez

Writing About the Big Question

Is conflict always bad?

Big Question Vocabulary

argue	battle	challenge	compete	conclude
convince	defend	game	issue	lose
negotiate	resist	resolve	survival	win

A. *Use one or more words from the list above to complete each sentence.*

1. When you are the new kid at school, the first day is a real _____.

2. You have to _____ to try to fit in and make friends.

3. You can _____ other kids that you are interesting and fun.

4. They will _____ that you would make a good friend.

B. *Respond to each item with a complete sentence.*

1. Describe an experience you have had being a new kid at school, or imagine what it would be like.

   _____

   _____

2. Tell what you did or would do at a new school to make friends. Use at least two Big Question vocabulary words in your response.

   _____

C. *Complete this sentence. Then, write a brief paragraph in which you connect this experience to the Big Question.*

   When I talk through conflicts with my family, _____.

   _____

   _____

   _____

   _____

   _____

   _____

"The Circuit" by Francisco Jiménez

Reading: Draw Conclusions

A conclusion is a decision or an opinion based on details in a literary work. To **identify the details** that will help you draw conclusions, **ask questions,** such as

- Why is this detail included in the story?
- Does this information help me understand the story better?

Example from "The Circuit":

The thought of having to move to Fresno and knowing what was in store for me there brought tears to my eyes.

You might ask what the narrator expects to happen in Fresno. The thought brings tears to his eyes. You can draw the conclusion that something in Fresno makes him sad.

A. DIRECTIONS: *The following passages from "The Circuit" are told from Panchito's point of view. Use details from each passage to draw a conclusion to answer the question.*

1. Suddenly I noticed Papa's face turn pale as he looked down the road. "Here comes the school bus," he whispered loudly in alarm. Instinctively, Roberto and I ran and hid in the vineyards.
   Does Papa want Roberto and Panchito to go to school? How do you know? _____

   _____

2. He walked up to me, handed me an English book, and asked me to read. "We are on page 125," he said politely. When I heard this, I felt my blood rush to my head; I felt dizzy.
   What makes Panchito feel dizzy? _____

   _____

3. Mr. Lema was sitting at his desk correcting papers. When I entered he looked up at me and smiled. I felt better. I walked up to him and asked if he could help me with the new words.
   How does Panchito feel about asking the teacher for help? _____

   _____

B. DIRECTIONS: *Underline details in this passage from "The Circuit" that help you draw the conclusion that the family is preparing to move. Then tell why these details help you draw this conclusion.*

I thought they were happy to see me, but when I opened the door to our shack, I saw that everything we owned was neatly packed in cardboard boxes.

Conclusion:

_____

_____

Name _____ Date _____

"The Circuit" by Francisco Jiménez

Literary Analysis: Theme

The **theme,** or central idea of a story, is a thought about life that the story conveys. Sometimes the theme is stated directly. Other times you must figure it out by considering events in the story, characters' thoughts and feelings, and the story's title.

A. DIRECTIONS: *Write a statement about the theme of "The Circuit."*

Theme: _____

_____

B. DIRECTIONS: *In the chart below, write the details from each passage that tell about or support the theme of "The Circuit." The first one is started for you as an example.*

Passage From "The Circuit"	What the Details Tell About Theme
1. Yes, it was that time of year. When I opened the front door to the shack, I stopped. Everything we owned was neatly packed in cardboard boxes. Suddenly I felt even more the weight of hours, days, weeks, and months of work.	The word *shack* indicates that the family is poor. Packed boxes indicate a change or move.
2. He was not going to school today. He was not going tomorrow, or next week, or next month. He would not go until the cotton season was over, . . .	
3. I thought they were happy to see me, but when I opened the door to our shack, I saw that everything we owned was neatly packed in cardboard boxes.	

"The Circuit" by Francisco Jiménez
Vocabulary Builder

Word List

accompanied   drone   enroll   instinctively   savoring

A. DIRECTIONS: *Each sentence below features a word from the list. For each sentence, explain why the underlined word does or does not make sense in the sentence.*

1. The <u>drone</u> of the television made it hard to concentrate.

   _____

2. Megan went home after school so she could <u>enroll</u> in a school club.

   _____

3. Carlos <u>instinctively</u> ducked when the ball came toward his face.

   _____

4. Jaime ate so fast he almost choked, <u>savoring</u> every bite.

   _____

5. Maria <u>accompanied</u> her father to the soccer match.

   _____

B. WORD STUDY: *The Latin prefix com- means "with," "together," or "next to." Answer each question by paying attention to each of the underlined words with the prefix com-. Then, explain your answer.*

1. Could you <u>combine</u> peanut butter and jelly to make a sandwich?

   _____

2. Could a pet ever be a good <u>companion</u> for a lonely person?

   _____

3. If you <u>compress</u> the items in a suitcase, is it harder to close it?

   _____

"The Circuit" by Francisco Jiménez
Conventions: Pronoun Case

Pronoun case is the form a pronoun takes to show how the pronoun is being used in a sentence. The three cases are **nominative, objective,** and **possessive**. The following chart shows each of the three pronoun cases and how it is used.

Pronoun Cases	How They Function	Examples
Nominative I, you, he, she, it, we, you, they	Nominative pronouns can act as subjects of a sentence or clause or as predicate pronouns (following a linking verb).	**Subjects:** <u>We</u> will go to the lab, where <u>they</u> are waiting. **Predicate Pronoun:** The first volunteer was <u>he</u>.
Objective me, you, him, her, it, us, them	Objective pronouns can act as direct or indirect objects or objects of a preposition.	**Direct Object:** Leah asked <u>us</u>. **Indirect Object:** Ms. Ang told <u>them</u> the scores. **Objects of a Preposition:** The interviewer will sit *across* from <u>you</u> and <u>me</u>.
Possessive my, mine, your, yours, his, her, hers, its, our, ours, their, theirs	Possessive pronouns show ownership. (Possessive pronouns that end in *s* never use an apostrophe.)	That cell phone is <u>hers</u>. No, <u>her</u> cell phone is silver. <u>Our</u> game is at 4:00; <u>theirs</u> is at 6:30. The show is in <u>its</u> third season.

A. PRACTICE: *Underline the pronoun in each sentence. Then on the line provided, write whether it is* Nominative (N), Objective (O), *or* Possessive (P) *case.*

_____ 1. Panchito took his trumpet home.

_____ 2. He wanted to show the trumpet to Carlos.

_____ 3. Mama gave him a pat on the head.

_____ 4. The boys collected the trash and put it in the container.

_____ 5. Panchito saw that the packed boxes were theirs.

_____ 6. The new students on the bus were we.

B. WRITING APPLICATION: *Describe a conversation between friends making plans for a Saturday afternoon. Use all three cases of pronouns in your paragraph. Underline each pronoun, and identify its case by writing* N, O, *or* P *above it.*

_____

_____

_____

_____

"The Circuit" by Francisco Jiménez

Support for Writing to Sources: Character Description

Choose a character from "The Circuit." Then, use the chart below to list details that describe that character. Include information from the story that illustrates the details used.

Name of Character: _____

Details That Describe the Character	Examples From the Story

Use the details that describe the character and examples from the story to write your character description.

Name _____ Date _____

"The Circuit" by Francisco Jiménez
Support for Speaking and Listening: Interview

With your partner, prepare to role-play an interview between a reporter and a migrant worker. The worker can be the main character or any other character in "The Circuit." Write questions and answers that you can use in your interview.

Name of worker being interviewed _____

1. Questions about the person's age and family:

   Questions: _____

   _____

   _____

   Answers: _____

   _____

   _____

   _____

2. Questions about the person's observations on American life:

   Questions: _____

   _____

   _____

   Answers: _____

   _____

   _____

   _____

3. Questions about the person's favorite things:

   Questions: _____

   _____

   _____

   Answers: _____

   _____

   _____

   _____

"Lob's Girl" by Joan Aiken
"Jeremiah's Song" by Walter Dean Myers
Writing About the Big Question

 Is conflict always bad?

Big Question Vocabulary

argue	battle	challenge	compete	conclude
convince	defend	game	issue	lose
negotiate	resist	resolve	survival	win

A. *Use one or more words from the list above to complete each sentence.*

1. To journey 400 miles on foot is a real _____.

2. Lob's _____ on that long journey is amazing.

3. Ellie began to _____ Grandpa's storytelling when she returned from college.

4. Grandpa seemed to _____ Macon that the stories were worth keeping alive.

B. *Respond to each item with a complete sentence.*

1. Describe an experience you have had with a lost pet, or imagine what it would be like.

_____

_____

2. Explain what you did, or would do, to find a lost pet. Use at least two Big Question vocabulary words in your response.

_____

_____

C. *Complete this sentence. Then, write a brief paragraph in which you connect this experience to the Big Question.*

When family members have conflicts, they may find it hard to _____.

_____

_____

_____

_____

_____

_____

Name _____   Date _____

"Lob's Girl" by Joan Aiken
"Jeremiah's Song" by Walter Dean Myers
Literary Analysis: Plot Techniques

Writers can use a range of **plot techniques** to help them tell the events in a story. Two common plot techniques are foreshadowing and flashback.

- **Foreshadowing** is the author's use of clues to hint at what might happen later in the story. For example, a story's narrator might describe a sign that reads *Danger* hanging on a fence. This detail might suggest that something dangerous will happen later in the story. It also helps the author build suspense, the quality that keeps you wondering what will happen next.
- A **flashback** is a scene that interrupts a story to describe an earlier event. Flashback is often used to show something about a character's past. For example, a flashback about the loss of a special pet might explain why a character dislikes the new family dog.

DIRECTIONS: *Read each of the following passages from "Lob's Girl" and "Jeremiah's Song." Then, complete the sentence that follows.*

1. **from "Lob's Girl"**

   A. [Aunt Rebecca] found the family with white shocked faces; Bert and Jean were about to drive off to the hospital where Sandy had been taken, and the twins were crying bitterly. <u>Lob was nowhere to be seen</u>.

   The underlined detail foreshadows _____.

   B. The twins were miserably unhappy. They forgot that they had sometimes called their elder sister bossy and only remembered how often she had shared her pocket money with them, how she read to them and took them for picnics and helped with their homework.

   From the flashback in this paragraph, you learn that _____
   _____.

2. **from "Jeremiah's Song"**

   A. Grandpa Jeremiah had been feeling poorly from that stroke, and one of his legs got a little drag to it. Just about the time Ellie come from school the next summer he was real sick.

   This description of Grandpa foreshadows _____.

   B. When the work for the day was finished and the sows fed, Grandpa would kind of ease into one of his stories and Macon, he would sit and listen to them and be real interested.

   This flashback about Macon tells the reader that _____
   _____.

"Lob's Girl" by Joan Aiken
"Jeremiah's Song" by Walter Dean Myers
Vocabulary Builder

Word List

decisively   diagnosis   melancholy   resolutions

A. DIRECTIONS: *Revise each sentence so that the underlined vocabulary word is used logically. Be sure to keep the vocabulary word in your revision.*

Sentence: After I told her every detail, Mom thanked me for the <u>summary</u>.

Revision: Mom thanked me for the brief <u>summary</u> of what had happened.

1. Unsure what to do with the ball, Aaron threw it <u>decisively</u> to first base.

   _____

   _____

2. Our club could not decide what to do, so we were able to make good <u>resolutions</u> for the coming year.

   _____

   _____

3. The story's funny, happy ending made Li feel <u>melancholy</u>.

   _____

   _____

4. After the vet's clear <u>diagnosis</u>, we still didn't know what was wrong with Spot.

   _____

   _____

B. DIRECTIONS: *Write the letter of the word that means the same or almost the same as the vocabulary word.*

____ 1. melancholy
   A. depressed
   B. peaceful
   C. sweet
   D. mean

____ 2. diagnosis
   A. speech
   B. measurement
   C. disease
   D. conclusion

____ 3. resolutions
   A. apologies
   B. guesses
   C. promises
   D. chores

Name _____ Date _____

"Lob's Girl" by Joan Aiken
"Jeremiah's Song" by Walter Dean Myers
Support for Writing to Compare Literary Works

Before you draft your essay comparing and contrasting the authors' use of foreshadowing and flashback in these stories, complete the graphic organizers below.

Foreshadowing	
Examples from "Lob's Girl"	**Examples from "Jeremiah's Song"**
Which story's foreshadowing creates greater suspense? Why?	

Flashback	
Examples from "Lob's Girl"	**Examples from "Jeremiah's Song"**
Which story's flashbacks reveal more about its characters? How?	

Now, use your notes to write an essay comparing and contrasting the authors' use of foreshadowing and flashback in these two stories. Remember to tell which story you enjoyed more and why.

Name _____   Date _____

Support for Writing a Narrative: Short Story

Prewriting: Narrowing Your Topic

Answer the questions in the following chart to help identify the conflict of your story.

What does my main character want?	
Who or what is getting in the way?	
What will the character do to overcome the person or thing that is getting in the way?	

Drafting: Developing a Plot

Use the following graphic organizer to organize the plot, or sequence of events, in your short story.

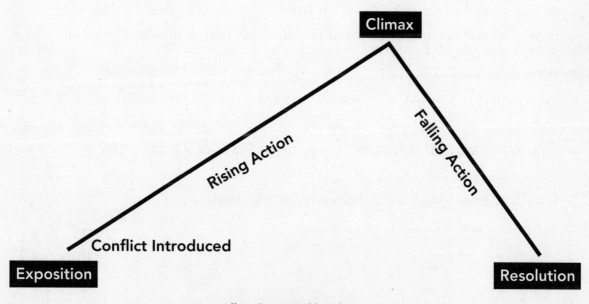

Name _____ Date _____

Conventions: Pronoun-Antecedent Agreement

An antecedent is a noun to which a pronoun refers. For example, in this sentence, *Luisa* is the antecedent, and *she* is the pronoun: Luisa said that she passed the test. The pronoun must agree in number, person, and gender.

Antecedent	Example	Rule	Example Sentence
singular noun	boy, girl, table	Use a singular pronoun.	The **boy** walked **his** dog.
plural noun	boys, girls, tables	Use a plural pronoun.	The **girls** rehearsed **their** speeches.
first-person	Ana, I Ana and I	Use first-person pronouns.	Ana said, "<u>I</u> will be on time." Ana and I said, "<u>We</u> will be on time."
third-person	Ana and she	Use a third-person pronoun.	Ana and she said that <u>they</u> would be on time.
third-person male	Ben	Use a third-person male pronoun.	Ben said <u>he</u> was sorry to be late.
third-person female	Addy	Use a third-person female pronoun.	Addy said that <u>she</u> didn't have to wait very long.

Using Pronoun/Antecedent Agreement

A. PRACTICE: *Circle the pronoun that correctly completes each sentence.*

1. The waitress took out (*their, her*) notepad to take our order.

2. Both boys wanted milkshakes with (*their, his*) sandwiches.

3. Damon ordered onions and mustard on (*their, his*) sandwich.

B. WRITING APPLICATION: *Follow the instructions on each line below.*

1. *Write a sentence using a singular noun and singular pronoun.*

   _____

2. *Write a sentence in the first person, using a first-person pronoun.*

   _____

3. *Write a sentence using a third-person female pronoun.*

   _____

"The King of Mazy May," by Jack London
Vocabulary Builder

Selection Vocabulary

endured   liable   summit

A. DIRECTIONS: *Decide whether each statement below is true or false. On the line before each item, write TRUE or FALSE. Then explain your answers.*

_____ 1. If you are *liable* to do something, that means you probably won't do it.

_____

_____ 2. When hikers arrive at the *summit* of a hill, they have reached the top.

_____

_____ 3. A person who *endured* hardships could not tolerate the hardships and gave up.

_____

Academic Vocabulary

alter   contribute   passage

B. DIRECTIONS: *Write the answer to each question on the line provided.*

1. What may cause travelers to *alter* their plans?

_____

2. For what reason might you not *contribute* to a conversation about a new movie?

_____

3. Is a *passage* from a story the whole story? Explain your answer.

_____

Name _____ Date _____

"The King of Mazy May," by Jack London
Take Notes for Discussion

Before the Group Discussion: Read the passage from the selection in your textbook.

Walt Masters is not a very large boy, but there is manliness in his make-up, and he himself, although he does not know a great deal that most boys know, knows much that other boys do not know. He has never seen a train of cars nor an elevator in his life, and for that matter he has never once looked upon a cornfield, a plow, a cow, or even a chicken. He has never had a pair of shoes on his feet, nor gone to a picnic or a party, nor talked to a girl. But he has seen the sun at midnight, watched the ice jams on one of the mightiest of rivers, and played beneath the northern lights, the one white child in thousands of square miles of frozen wilderness.

During the Discussion: As the group discusses each question, take notes on how other students' ideas either differ from or build upon your own.

Discussion Questions	Other Responses	Comparison to My Responses
1. How does the author compare Walt's experiences with those of other boys?		
2. What do the details in this passage tell you about the narrator's attitude toward Walt?		
3. In what way is Walt well suited to the challenges of his environment and circumstance?		

Name _____ Date _____

"The King of Mazy May," by Jack London

Take Notes for Writing to Sources

Planning Your Informative Text: Before you begin drafting your **cause-and-effect essay,** use the diagram below to organize your ideas.

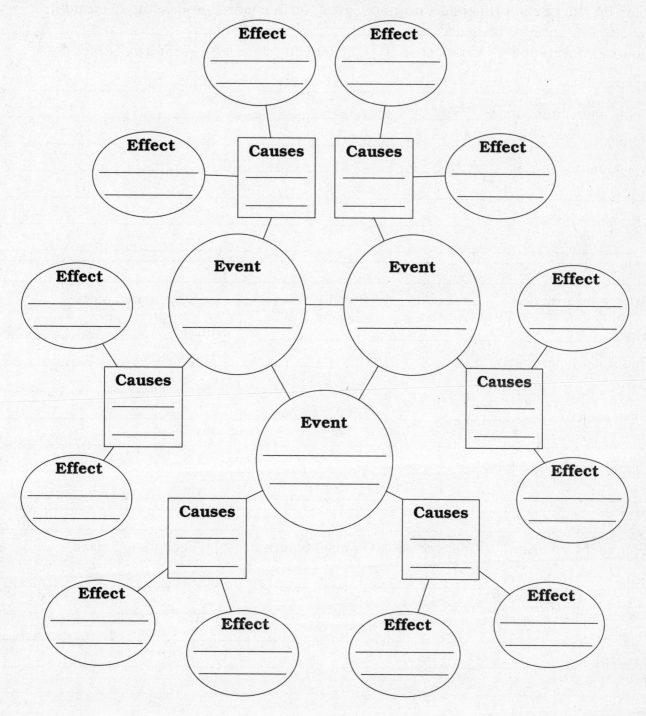

Name _____ Date _____

Take Notes for Research

As you research **the living conditions for gold prospectors in Canada in the 1890s,** use the forms below to take notes from your sources. As necessary, continue your notes on the back of this page, on note cards, or in a word-processing document.

Source Information   Check one: ☐ Primary Source   ☐ Secondary Source

Title: _____   Author: _____

Publication Information: _____

Page(s): _____

Main Idea: _____

_____

Quotation or Paraphrase: _____

_____

Source Information   Check one: ☐ Primary Source   ☐ Secondary Source

Title: _____   Author: _____

Publication Information: _____

Page(s): _____

Main Idea: _____

_____

Quotation or Paraphrase: _____

_____

Source Information   Check one: ☐ Primary Source   ☐ Secondary Source

Title: _____   Author: _____

Publication Information: _____

Page(s): _____

Main Idea: _____

_____

Quotation or Paraphrase: _____

_____

"To Klondyke We've Paid Our Fare," written and composed H. J. Dunham
Vocabulary Builder

Selection Vocabulary

defiance   invincible   privation

A. DIRECTIONS: *Write at least one synonym, one antonym, and an example sentence for each word. Synonyms and antonyms can be words or phrases.*

Word	Synonym	Antonym	Example Sentence
defiance			
invincible			
privation			

Academic Vocabulary

challenge   purpose   reveal

B. DIRECTIONS: *Write a response to each question. Make sure to use the italicized word at least once in your response.*

1. Why might someone *challenge* a friend to join him on a trip to the Klondyke?

    _____

    _____

2. What is the *purpose* of the "Argonauts" who journey to the Klondyke? Explain.

    _____

    _____

3. In your opinion, what do the lyrics of this song *reveal* about the characters of the people who travel to the Klondyke?

    _____

Name _____ Date _____

"To Klondyke We've Paid Our Fare," written and composed H. J. Dunham
Take Notes for Discussion

Before the discussion: Read the following passage from the selection.

> **Refrain:** To Klondyke we've paid our fare,
> our golden slippers we soon will wear.
> We'll live on pig and polar bear, and gather
> the nuggets we know are there.

During the Discussion: As you discuss each question, take notes on how other students' ideas either differ from or build upon your own.

Discussion Questions	Other Ideas Expressed	Comparison to My Own Ideas
1. How would you describe the mood of the song's refrain?		
2. Why might a song like this have been popular with Gold Rush settlers?		

"To Klondyke We've Paid Our Fare," written and composed by H. J. Dunham
Take Notes for Research

As you research **the Klondike Gold Rush,** use the chart below to take notes from your sources. As necessary, continue your notes on the back of this page, on note cards, or in a word-processing document.

Source Information   Check one: ☐ Primary Source   ☐ Secondary Source

Title: _____   Author: _____

Publication Information: _____

Page(s): _____

Main Idea: _____

_____

Quotation or Paraphrase: _____

_____

Source Information   Check one: ☐ Primary Source   ☐ Secondary Source

Title: _____   Author: _____

Publication Information: _____

Page(s): _____

Main Idea: _____

_____

Quotation or Paraphrase: _____

_____

Source Information   Check one: ☐ Primary Source   ☐ Secondary Source

Title: _____   Author: _____

Publication Information: _____

Page(s): _____

Main Idea: _____

_____

Quotation or Paraphrase: _____

_____

"To Klondyke We've Paid Our Fare," written and composed by H. J. Dunham
Take Notes for Writing to Sources

Planning Your Narrative: Before you begin drafting your **short story,** use the chart below to organize your ideas.

1. Details about your character and the setting:
2. Progression of events that build on one another:
3. Information from your research:
4. Details about your conclusion:

Gold Rush: The Journey by Land
Vocabulary Builder and Writing to Sources

Selection Vocabulary

pioneers   severe

A. DIRECTIONS: *Write two sentences describing the hardships facing the people traveling west overland. Use one or both vocabulary words in each sentence.*

1. _____

2. _____

Academic Vocabulary

indicated   process   similarities

B. DIRECTIONS: *Write a response to each question. Make sure to use the italicized word at least once in your response.*

1. Describe a *process* that you have used or that you use regularly. _____

_____

2. On the annotated map in your textbook, what is *indicated* by small, black dots?

_____

_____

3. Describe the *similarities* between two people you know.

_____

Writing to Sources: Journal Entry

As you plan your **journal entry,** use the chart below as a guide.

The character from whose point of view I will be writing: _____	
A description of the site where the character's experiences take place	
The character's experiences at the site	

Name _____ Date _____

"A Woman's View of the Gold Rush," by Mary Ballou
Vocabulary Builder

Selection Vocabulary

associate   scouring   tongues

A. DIRECTIONS: *Write one example of people, things, or actions that demonstrate the meaning of each word. Follow this example.*

RUDIMENTS: basic tasks, such as the steps in boiling an egg

1. ASSOCIATE: _____

2. SCOURING: _____

3. TONGUES: _____

Academic Vocabulary

abandons   reflect   specific

B. DIRECTIONS: *Follow each direction. Write each response in a full sentence.*

1. Describe the actions of a committee member who *abandons* good manners. _____

_____

2. How does a person's style of clothing *reflect* his or her personality? _____

_____

_____

3. Is it helpful to police to have a *specific* description of a criminal? Why or why not?

_____

_____

"A Woman's View of the Gold Rush," by Mary Ballou
Take Notes for Discussion

Before the Partner Discussion: Read the following passage from the selection.

> Somtimes, I am taking care of Babies and nursing at the rate of Fifty Dollars a week but I would not advise any Lady to come out here and suffer the toil and fatigue that I have suffered for the sake of a little gold neither do I advise any one to come. Clarks Simmon wife says if she was safe in the States she would not care if she had not one cent.

During the Discussion: As you discuss each question, take notes on how your partner's ideas either differ from or build upon your own.

Discussion Questions	My Partner's Ideas	Comparison to My Own Ideas
1. Has Mary Ballou been successful in California? Cite specific details from the passage to support your answer.		
2. California was a state in 1852. Explain the meaning of the comment by Clark Simmon's wife about being "safe in the States."		

Name _____ Date _____

"A Woman's View of the Gold Rush," by Mary Ballou
Take Notes for Research

As you research **housing during the Gold Rush,** you can use the forms below. As necessary, continue your notes on the back of this page, on note cards, or in a word-processing document.

Source Information   Check one: ☐ Primary Source   ☐ Secondary Source

Title: _____   Author: _____

Publication Information: _____

Page(s): _____

Main Idea: _____

_____

Quotation or Paraphrase: _____

_____

Source Information   Check one: ☐ Primary Source   ☐ Secondary Source

Title: _____   Author: _____

Publication Information: _____

Page(s): _____

Main Idea: _____

_____

Quotation or Paraphrase: _____

_____

Source Information   Check one: ☐ Primary Source   ☐ Secondary Source

Title: _____   Author: _____

Publication Information: _____

Page(s): _____

Main Idea: _____

_____

Quotation or Paraphrase: _____

_____

Name _____ Date _____

Planning your informational text: Before you begin drafting your informational text, use the chart below to organize your ideas.

1. Topic of the text: _____ _____
2. Women's duties and jobs during the Gold Rush: _____ _____ _____ _____ _____ _____
3. Specific information from the text that can lead to generalizations: _____ _____ _____ _____ _____ _____ _____ _____ _____ _____
4. Summary of ideas for your conclusion: _____ _____ _____ _____

All-in-One Workbook
51

"Chinese and African Americans in the Gold Rush"
Vocabulary Builder

Selection Vocabulary

    ambassador   exodus   testify

A. DIRECTIONS: *Write the letter of the word or phrase that is the best synonym for the italicized word. Then use the italicized word in a complete sentence.*

_____ 1. *ambassador*

    A. gold miner   **C.** special representative

    B. immigrant   **D.** slave

_____

_____ 2. *exodus*

    A. musical instrument   **C.** examination

    B. trial by jury   **D.** departure

_____

_____ 3. *testify*

    A. be a witness in court   **C.** free slaves

    B. give tests   **D.** interview for a job

_____

Academic Vocabulary

    acquired   determine

B. DIRECTIONS: *Complete each sentence with a word, phrase, or clause that contains a context clue for the italicized word.*

1. Knowledge is usually *acquired* by _____

_____.

2. You can *determine* the best route for getting from one place to another by _____

_____.

Name _____ Date _____

"Chinese and African Americans in the Gold Rush"
Take Notes for Discussion

Before the Group Discussion: Read the following passage from the selection.

Many African Americans came to California as well. They hoped to find freedom and good jobs. Most were free men and women from eastern cities. Some free African Americans had fled the east to escape the Fugitive Slave Law.

During the Discussion: As you discuss each question, take notes on how your group members' ideas either differ from or build upon your own.

Discussion Questions	Other Ideas Expressed	Comparison to My Own Ideas
1. How did slavery affect the Gold Rush?		
2. What issues motivated African American workers to travel west?		

All-in-One Workbook
53

Name _____ Date _____

Take Notes for Research

As you research the **process of mining and panning for gold,** you can use the organizer below to take notes from your sources. As necessary, continue your notes on the back of this page, on note cards, or in a word-processing document.

Source Information   Check one: ☐ Primary Source   ☐ Secondary Source

Title: _____   Author: _____

Publication Information: _____

Page(s): _____

Main Idea: _____

_____

Quotation or Paraphrase: _____

_____

Source Information   Check one: ☐ Primary Source   ☐ Secondary Source

Title: _____   Author: _____

Publication Information: _____

Page(s): _____

Main Idea: _____

_____

Quotation or Paraphrase: _____

_____

Source Information   Check one: ☐ Primary Source   ☐ Secondary Source

Title: _____   Author: _____

Publication Information: _____

Page(s): _____

Main Idea: _____

_____

Quotation or Paraphrase: _____

_____

Name _____ Date _____

Planning Your Editorial: Before you begin drafting your **editorial,** use the chart below to organize your ideas.

---

1. Your position on the issue:

_____

_____

_____

_____

_____

---

2. Facts and details to support your position and claims:

_____

_____

_____

_____

_____

_____

_____

_____

_____

_____

_____

_____

_____

---

3. Transitional words and phrases to clarify the relationships among ideas:

_____

_____

_____

_____

_____

_____

_____

Name _____ Date _____

"Birds Struggle to Recover from Egg Thefts of 1800s" by Edie Lau
Vocabulary Builder

Selection Vocabulary

conservatively   entrepreneurs   faltered

A. DIRECTIONS: *Write the letter of the word or phrase that is the best synonym for the italicized word. Then use the italicized word in a complete sentence.*

_____ 1. *conservatively*

    A. thoughtfully   **C.** cautiously

    B. in a stern manner   **D.** loosely

_____

_____ 2. *entrepreneurs*

    A. species of bird   **C.** egg collectors

    B. businesspeople   **D.** doctors

_____

_____ 3. *faltered*

    A. disappeared   **C.** moved

    B. grew   **D.** weakened

_____

Academic Vocabulary

establish   opinion   support

B. DIRECTIONS: *Following the directions, answer each question in a complete sentence.*

1. Name something that would *establish* the truth of an alibi. _____

_____

2. Describe two aspects of a story that would help you form a good or bad *opinion* of it.

_____

_____

3. In what way might a voter *support* a candidate for office? _____

_____

Name _____ Date _____

Before the Group Discussion: Read the following passage from the selection.

The Farallon Islands and surrounding ocean make a rich marine environment. The islands are known as the largest sea bird rookery in the continental United States. The Farallons are alive and noisy with seagulls, puffins, auklets, and cormorants, to name a few; the air is thick with the pungent scent of their guano. Sea lions and seals lounge on ledges or cavort in caves.

The Farallons' abundant wildlife impressed Yankee seamen and Russian explorers in the early nineteenth century. They hunted the seals for their pelts, meat, and blubber.

During the Discussion: As the group discusses each question, take notes on how other students' ideas either differ from or build upon your own.

Discussion Questions	Other Ideas Expressed	Comparison to My Own Ideas
1. How do the words the writer uses to describe the Farallon Islands suggest her attitude toward the subject?		
2. Contrast the ways the islands' wildlife impresses the writer and the explorers.		

Name _____ Date _____

"Birds Struggle to Recover from Egg Thefts of 1800s" by Edie Lau
Take Notes for Research

As you research **the types of food miners and their families ate during the Gold Rush,** you can use the organizer below to take notes from your sources. As necessary, continue your notes on the back of this page, on note cards, or in a word-processing document.

Source Information   Check one: ☐ Primary Source   ☐ Secondary Source

Title: _____   Author: _____

Publication Information: _____

Page(s): _____

Main Idea: _____

_____

Quotation or Paraphrase: _____

_____

Source Information   Check one: ☐ Primary Source   ☐ Secondary Source

Title: _____   Author: _____

Publication Information: _____

Page(s): _____

Main Idea: _____

_____

Quotation or Paraphrase: _____

_____

Source Information   Check one: ☐ Primary Source   ☐ Secondary Source

Title: _____   Author: _____

Publication Information: _____

Page(s): _____

Main Idea: _____

_____

Quotation or Paraphrase: _____

_____

Name _____ Date _____

"Birds Struggle to Recover from Egg Thefts of 1800s" by Edie Lau
Take Notes for Writing to Sources

Planning Your Argument: Before you begin drafting your **argument,** use the chart below to organize your ideas.

1. Notes for your introduction to the problem or issue:

_____

_____

_____

_____

_____

2. Your opinion:

_____

_____

_____

_____

_____

_____

_____

_____

_____

_____

_____

_____

3. Evidence from the article to support your position:

_____

_____

_____

_____

_____

_____

Name _____ Date _____

Unit 2: Types of Nonfiction
Big Question Vocabulary—1

The Big Question: What is important to know?

Often, in order to learn about something, we must put in some effort. The words that follow are used to describe that effort.

concept: an idea of how something is or how something should be done

examine: to look carefully at something in order to learn more about it

knowledge: the information and understanding that you have gained through learning and experience

question: a sentence used to ask for information

study: *n.* a piece of work done to find out more about a subject or problem; *v.* to watch and examine something carefully over a period of time to find out more about it

DIRECTIONS: *Complete the blanks in the story that follows using the vocabulary words above. You will use all of the words, some of them more than once.*

Ms. Walsh was talking about some scientific (1) _____ that Derrick did

not understand. He raised his hand to ask Ms. Walsh a (2) _____ .

"Yes, Derrick?" Ms. Walsh called on him.

"I do not understand that (3) _____, Ms. Walsh," Derrick said.

"Well," said Ms. Walsh, "Let's (4) _____ your (5) _____,

Derrick. Have you been paying attention to what has been going on in class today?"

Derrick's face reddened and he shook his head. He had been distracted.

"It's okay, Derrick," said Ms. Walsh. "If you (6) _____ pages 32-34 in

the science textbook tonight, you will gain the same (7) _____ that the rest

of the class gained in our class discussion today."

DIRECTIONS: *Answer the following question in full sentences, using at least three of the vocabulary words in your answer.*

8. You discover an interesting yellow and green insect in your backyard. It is about the size and shape of your pinky finger and it has many legs. You really want to know more about this insect. What do you do?

_____

_____

_____

Unit 2: Types of Nonfiction
Big Question Vocabulary—2

The Big Question: What is important to know?

How do we form our opinions? Sometimes our opinions are based on knowledge, and sometimes they are based on an instinct or a feeling. It is important to be open to learning facts that might change your opinion.

distinguish: to recognize or understand the difference between two similar things or people

guess: to answer a question or make a judgment without knowing all the facts

judge: to form or give an opinion about something or someone

observe: to watch someone or something carefully in order to learn something

purpose: the aim or result that an activity or event is supposed to achieve

How do you choose your friends?

Write sentences in the chart below describing how some people might choose friends on each basis listed. Use the word in parentheses in your sentences. Put a star next to the way that you like to choose friends.

Some people choose friends based on:	
1. their hobbies **(distinguish)**	
2. how they look **(judge)**	
3. what they see others doing or hear them saying **(observe)**	
4. what they might want to learn from others **(purpose)**	
5. a feeling **(guess)**	

All-in-One Workbook
61

Name _____ Date _____

Unit 2: Types of Nonfiction
Big Question Vocabulary—3

The Big Question: What is important to know?

There is so much information available in so many forms that sometimes it is difficult to determine which information is useful to you and which information should be disregarded.

limit: the greatest or least amount of something that is allowed

measure: to judge something's importance, value, size, weight, or true nature

narrow: limited in scope or amount

refer: to mention or speak about someone or something

source: a person, book, or document that supplies you with information

DIRECTIONS: *Read the passage. Then, complete the list below, using the words in parentheses.*

You have been assigned a research project. You are to research the state where you live. You get on the Internet and you begin to do your research, but there is so much information! What should you do?

Make a list of strategies to help you figure out what to include.

1. (narrow) *In order to make this report manageable, I will* _____

_____

2. (limit, source) *When researching, I will make sure to* _____

_____

_____

3. (measure) *I have to remember to* _____

_____

_____

4. (refer) *I will not* _____

_____

Name _____ Date _____

Unit 2: Types of Nonfiction
Applying the Big Question

 What is important to know?

DIRECTIONS: Complete the chart below to apply what you have learned about what is important to know. One row has been completed for you.

Example	Something important to know	Source of this knowledge	Why knowing this is important	Ways this knowledge can be used	What I learned
From Literature	It is terrible to live in a war zone.	*Zlata's Diary*	Even if you yourself are never in a war, you can understand what it is like.	to understand kids who live in places where wars are happening today	Wars are not just events in history—they happen to people who are alive right now.
From Literature					
From Science					
From Social Studies					
From Real Life					

Name _____ Date _____

Writing About the Big Question

What is important to know?

Big Question Vocabulary

concept	distinguish	examine	guess	judge
knowledge	limit	measure	narrow	observe
purpose	question	refer	source	study

A. *Use one or more words from the list above to complete the following sentences.*

1. If someone is nice to you only when he or she has something to gain, you may
_____ that that person is not really nice.

2. If someone's words do not match his or her actions, you might want to
_____ what that person is really like.

3. We can use evidence to _____ what is fact from what is opinion.

4. You should always _____ your opinions to see whether or not they
are true.

B. *Respond to each item. Use at least two Big Question vocabulary words in each
answer.*

1. Describe a time when somebody you thought was a good person did something that
was not nice.

_____

_____

2. After the issue was resolved, did you determine that the person was a good person
or not? Explain.

_____

_____

C. *Complete the sentence below. Then, write a short paragraph connecting this situation
to the Big Question.*

A truly "extra good" person is _____

Is it true that somebody can be "extra good"? Or does everyone have a good side
and a bad side? How do you know?

_____

_____

_____

Name _____ Date _____

"The Drive-In Movies" by Gary Soto
Reading: Read Ahead to Verify Predictions

Predictions are reasonable guesses about what is most likely to happen next. Your predictions should be based on details in the literature and your own experience. After you have made a prediction, **read ahead to check your prediction.** Making and checking predictions improves your understanding by helping you notice and think about important details.

For example, at the beginning of "The Drive-In Movies," you might wonder if Gary's mom is going to take her children to the movies. You read the story clue that Mom might be tired from working all week. You know that when parents are tired they might want to get to bed early. You might predict that the children won't get to the movies. You keep reading and you find out at the end of the story if your prediction is right or wrong.

DIRECTIONS: *As you read "The Drive-In Movies," use the chart below to help you predict events in the story. First, read the question in column 1. Fill in column 2 with a story clue. In column 3, note information from your own experience. Then make a prediction in column 4. Finally, read to see if your prediction is correct. If your prediction is correct, write the letter C in the last column. If it is wrong, write the letter W.*

1. Question	2. Story Clue	3. What You Know from Experience	4. Prediction	C or W
Will Rick help?				
Will a good job be done on the car?				
How will Mom react to the way the car looks?				
Will Gary enjoy the movies?				

Name _____   Date _____

"The Drive-In Movies" by Gary Soto
Literary Analysis: Narrator and Point of View

The **narrator** is the voice that tells a true or imagined story. **Point of view** is the perspective from which the story is told. These two points of view are the most commonly used:

- **First-person point of view:** The narrator participates in the action of the story and refers to himself or herself as "I." Readers know only what the narrator sees, thinks, and feels.

  One Saturday I decided to be extra good.

- **Third-person point of view:** The narrator does not participate in the action of the story. A third-person narrator can tell things that the characters do not know.

  Rick, Gary, and Debra wanted their mother to love each of them best.

Most true stories about a person's life are told in first-person point of view.

A. DIRECTIONS: *If the sentence is spoken by a first-person narrator, write* FP *on the line. If the sentence is spoken by a third-person narrator, write* TP *on the line.*

____ 1. My knees hurt from kneeling, and my brain was dull from making the trowel go up and down, dribbling crumbs of earth.

____ 2. His knees hurt from kneeling, and his brain was dull from making the trowel go up and down, dribbling crumbs of earth.

____ 3. His brother joined him with an old gym sock, and their sister, happy not to join them, watched while sucking on a cherry Kool-Aid ice cube.

____ 4. My brother joined me with an old gym sock, and our sister watched us while sucking on a cherry Kool-Aid ice cube.

B. DIRECTIONS: *In the space provided below, rewrite the following paragraph with Mom as the first-person narrator. The first sentence is done for you.*

Mom came out and looked at the car. She saw that the waxed side was foggy white. The other side hadn't even been done. She said, "You boys worked so hard." She turned on the garden hose and washed off the soap her sons had not been able to get off. Even though she was tired from working all week, she took her children to the drive-in that night. She knew that Gary had worked most of Saturday. He had been extra good and he especially deserved a treat.

I went out and looked at the car.

_____

_____

_____

_____

"The Drive-In Movies" by Gary Soto
Vocabulary Builder

Word List

evident   migrated   prelude   pulsating   vigorously   winced

A. DIRECTIONS: *In each item below, think about the meaning of the underlined word. Look for clues in the rest of the sentence. Then, answer the question.*

1. If wild geese have <u>migrated</u> to your town for the winter, are they likely to stay all year? Why or why not?

_____

2. My dad <u>winced</u> when he buttoned his shirt collar. Was the collar too loose? Why or why not?

_____

3. If the identity of the thief is <u>evident</u> to everyone, will the police know who robbed the bank? Why or why not?

_____

4. Which part of the human body is always <u>pulsating</u>, the kidneys or the heart? Explain your answer, using a synonym for *pulsating*.

_____

5. John wanted to get someplace quickly. Would he walk <u>vigorously</u>? Why or why not?

_____

6. When the band plays the <u>prelude</u> to a piece of music, is the musical piece ending? Why or why not?

_____

B. WORD STUDY: The Latin prefix *pre-* means "before." Read each sentence. Decide whether it makes sense. If it does, write *Correct*. If it doesn't make sense, revise it so that it does.

1. After I wore my new jeans, I washed them to *preshrink* the fabric.

_____

2. The United States Constitution ends with a *preamble*.

_____

3. Early in the day, you can *precook* the main course and then reheat it in the microwave just before dinner is served.

_____

"The Drive-In Movies" by Gary Soto

Conventions: Principal Parts of Regular and Irregular Verbs

A verb is a word that expresses an action or a state of being. Every verb has four main forms, or **principal parts**. These parts show the tense of a verb. The tense lets you know when an action took place. Most verbs are **regular**, meaning that they form their principal parts in the same way. Some verbs, however, are **irregular**, meaning that the forms of their principal parts do not follow general rules. The principal parts of irregular verbs must be learned.

Principal Part	Regular Verbs	Irregular Verbs
Present tense	talk, jump, finish, expect	am/is/are, have/has, sing/sings, become/becomes, bring/brings
Past tense	Add -*ed*: talked, jumped, finished, expected	was/were, had, sang, became, brought
Present participle	Add -*ing*: (am/is/are/was/were) talking, jumping, finishing, expecting	(am/is/are/was/were) being, having, singing, becoming, bringing
Past participle	Add -*ed*: (has/have/had) talked, jumped, finished, expected	(has/have/had) been, had, sung, become, brought

A. PRACTICE: *For each of the following sentences, identify which principal part of the underlined verb is being used. The first one has been done as an example.*

_____past_____ 1. The sun <u>shone</u> for only a few hours that day.

_____ 2. Gary *is* <u>having</u> trouble staying awake at the drive-in.

_____ 3. Gary <u>knows</u> that if he is good, the family will go to the drive-in.

_____ 4. His brother *has* <u>helped</u> him wax the car.

_____ 5. Gary *had* <u>spent</u> the day doing chores.

_____ 6. He *was* <u>hoping</u> to go to the drive-in that evening.

_____ 7. Gary's mother <u>understood</u> what the children were trying to do.

B. Writing Application: *Write a sentence using the verb and principal part indicated.*

1. decide; present tense

_____

2. become; past tense

_____

"The Drive-In Movies" by Gary Soto
Support for Writing to Sources: Autobiographical Narrative

For your autobiographical narrative, begin by making a timeline. Use the graphic organizer below to list chronologically a few important events in your life. On the diagonal lines, write a few words about big events or periods of time that you remember well. For example, you might write "moved to new school."

Timeline

Birth   **Now**

Choose an event from the timeline for your autobiographical narrative and write the event on the Event line below. Then list details about the event on the Details lines. Number the details in the order they occurred. Use your numbered list to help you write your autobiographical narrative.

Event _____

Details _____

_____

_____

_____

_____

_____

_____

_____

_____

_____

_____

_____

_____

Name _____ Date _____

"The Drive-In Movies" by Gary Soto
Support for Speaking and Listening: Conversation

With a partner, prepare to act out a converstion Gary Soto might have had with his mother the day after their trip to the drive-in.

1. Use the space below to write a few details you and your partner might include in your invented dialogue.

_____

_____

_____

_____

_____

_____

_____

_____

2. Use this space to jot down details about each character's traits, goals, and feelings. These notes will help you write stage directions to show how each character should speak. For example, you might write:

    Gary Soto: *(speaking softly)* That was hard work.

Character #1: (Name: _____)

_____

_____

Character #2: (Name: _____)

_____

_____

Now, with your partner, use these notes to act out the conversation for your class. Be sure to make eye contact and to use expressive tones of voice and gestures.

All-in-One Workbook
70

"Names/Nombres" by Julia Alvarez
Writing About the Big Question

What is important to know?

Big Question Vocabulary

concept	distinguish	examine	guess	judge
knowledge	limit	measure	narrow	observe
purpose	question	refer	source	study

A. *Use one or more words from the list above to complete the following sentences.*

1. If a friend is being unfriendly, I have to _____ why he is angry with me.

2. It makes me angry that a friend would _____ me for doing something wrong when I am innocent.

3. We can use evidence to _____ fact from opinion.

4. A wise person will _____ her opinions to see whether or not they are true.

B. *Respond to each item. Use at least one Big Question vocabulary word in each answer.*

1. Describe how you might confirm that a friend is not angry with you.

_____

_____

2. When you find something that someone tells you is unbelievable, what do you do to get at the truth?

_____

_____

C. *Complete the sentence below. Then, write a short paragraph connecting this situation to the Big Question.*

Sometimes it takes courage to show your true feelings because _____

_____

_____

_____

_____

"Names/Nombres" by Julia Alvarez
Reading: Fact and Opinion

In order to evaluate a work of nonfiction, you must understand the difference between fact and opinion. A **fact,** unlike an opinion, can be proved. An **opinion** expresses a judgment that can be supported but not proved. For example, the statement "The Dominican Republic is in the Caribbean Sea" is a fact that can be proved by observation. All you need to do is look at a map. The statement "The climate in the Dominican Republic is perfect" is a judgment based on the weather.

You can **check facts by using resources** such as

- dictionaries
- encyclopedias
- reliable Web sites on the Internet
- maps

A. DIRECTIONS: *Identify the following passages from or about "Names/Nombres" as fact or opinion. Write F if the statement is a fact and O if it is an opinion.*

____ 1. "We had been born in New York City when our parents had first tried immigration."

____ 2. The Dominican Republic is south of Bermuda.

____ 3. "It was the ugliest name she had ever heard."

____ 4. "Tía Josefina . . . was not really an aunt but a much older cousin."

____ 5. "Our goodbyes went on too long."

B. DIRECTIONS: *Each statement below contains an error. Name the resource you would consult to check the statement. (If you would consult a Web site, write the name of the site.) Then, look up the statement in that resource, and rewrite it correctly.*

1. Julia Alvarez moved to the United States for good in 1962.

   Fact-checking resource: _____ **Correction:** _____

   _____

2. Julia Alvarez wrote a book called *How the Alvarez Girls Lost Their Accents.*

   Fact-checking resource: _____ **Correction:** _____

   _____

3. The Dominican Republic is on the same island as Cuba.

   Fact-checking resource: _____ **Correction:** _____

   _____

4. Bermuda is an island in the Caribbean Sea.

   Fact-checking resource: _____ **Correction:** _____

   _____

"Names/Nombres" by Julia Alvarez
Literary Analysis: Tone

The **tone** of a literary work is the writer's attitude toward his or her audience and subject. The tone can often be described in one word, such as *playful, serious,* or *humorous.* Factors that contribute to the tone are word choice, sentence structure, and sentence length. Notice how the writer's word choice creates a friendly, informal tone:

By the time I was in high school, I was a popular kid, and it showed in my name.

Sometimes, as in "Names/Nombres," humorous ideas, exaggeration, and dialogue help create a casual, informal tone. Alvarez's use of contractions, such as *wouldn't* and *didn't,* also adds to the informal tone.

A. DIRECTIONS: *As you read "Names/Nombres," look for details that add to the essay's informal, humorous tone. On the spider diagram, write one example of each contributing factor.*

Informal word: _____

Mispronunciation of Spanish: _____

Untranslated Spanish word: _____

Exaggeration: _____

Humorous idea: _____

Sentence fragment: _____

Another informal word: _____

Contraction: _____

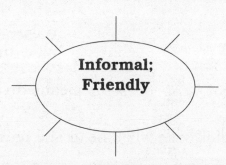

**Informal;
Friendly**

B. DIRECTIONS: *Read the following passage from "Names/Nombres." Underline three phrases or sentences that contribute to a relaxed, informal feeling. Then, rewrite the passage using a formal tone.*

At the hotel my mother was *Missus Alburest,* and I was little girl, as in, "Hey, *little girl,* stop riding the elevator up and down. It's *not* a toy."

Passage written in formal tone: _____

_____

_____

_____

Name _____ Date _____

"**Names/Nombres**" by Julia Alvarez
Vocabulary Builder

Word List

chaotic   inevitably   inscribed   mistook   pursue   transport

A. DIRECTIONS: *Write the letter of the word or phrase whose meaning is most nearly* the same as *the meaning of the Word List word.*

____ 1. inevitably
    A. finally
    B. unavoidably
    C. never
    D. invisibly

____ 2. chaotic
    A. confused
    B. noiseless
    C. tiny
    D. orderly

____ 3. transport
    A. bring in
    B. carry across
    C. send out
    D. extend

____ 4. mistook
    A. became lost or stolen
    B. made a mistake
    C. provided help
    D. bragged

____ 5. pursue
    A. follow or go after
    B. forget
    C. dream or imagine
    D. wish or hope for

____ 6. inscribed
    A. remembered
    B. sewn
    C. scratched
    D. written on

B. WORD STUDY: The Latin root *-scrib-* or *-scrip-* means "to write." Answer each question.

1. What message does a doctor write when he or she *prescribes* something?

_____

2. A *scriptorium* is a special room in a monastery. What activity do the monks do in this room?

_____

3. What *inscription* would you probably find on a birthday card?

_____

"Names/Nombres" by Julia Alvarez
Conventions: Action Verbs and Linking Verbs

A **verb** is a word that expresses the action or condition of a person, place, or thing. No sentence is complete without a verb. The two main kinds of verbs are action verbs and linking verbs.

    Action verbs express physical or mental action (*walk, sit, think*).

    Julia's family <u>moved</u> to the United States.

    Linking verbs express a state of being. They tell what the subject of a sentence is or is like by linking the subject to a word that further describes or identifies it. The most common linking verb is a form of *be* (*is, am, are,* and so on).

    The family <u>is</u> very poor.

    Other linking verbs include *appear, become, feel, seem, grow,* and *look.*

A. PRACTICE: *Underline the verbs in the following sentences. Then, above each one, write A if it is an action verb and L if it is a linking verb. Note that some of the sentences contain more than one verb.*

1. It was hard when we left our old home.
2. When we moved into the new apartment, the superintendent called my father *Mister Alberase.*
3. When I started school, my teachers called me by the wrong name.
4. I was a popular kid in school, and it showed in my name.
5. My mother felt awkward when she told her friends what she had named her first daughter.

B. Writing Application: *Follow the directions below to write sentences about the specified topics.*

1. Use the verb *feels* in a sentence about Julia.

_____

2. Use the verb *struggle* in a sentence about starting a new life.

_____

3. Use the verb *amazes* in a sentence about Julia's friends in high school.

_____

4. Use the verb *seems* in a sentence about arriving in New York City.

_____

5. Use the verb *moves* in a sentence about Julia's family.

_____

Name _____ Date _____

Support for Writing to Sources: Personal Anecdote

To prepare to write your anecdote, use this graphic organizer. First, name the experience you plan to write about. Then, in the left-hand column, write down the events that made up the experience. Write them in the order in which they happened. Finally, in the right-hand column, write your thoughts about each event.

The time when _____

Events	Thoughts About the Events
Key event in the beginning: _____ _____ _____ _____	_____ _____ _____ _____
Key event in the middle: _____ _____ _____ _____	_____ _____ _____ _____
Key event at most exciting moment: _____ _____ _____ _____	_____ _____ _____ _____
Key event at end: _____ _____ _____ _____	_____ _____ _____ _____

Now, use your notes to write your personal anecdote. Be sure to describe your thoughts about the experience.

"Names/Nombres" by Julia Alvarez
Support for Speaking and Listening: Monologue

Use the following questions to prepare to write and deliver a monologue presenting the thoughts of young Julia Alvarez when she first hears her name mispronounced. Imagine what you (Alvarez) might think.

- How do you feel the first time you hear your name mispronounced?

_____

_____

_____

_____

- What thoughts do you have the first time you hear your name mispronounced? (Describe at least three thoughts. Remember to use the first-person point of view and the pronoun *I*.)

1. _____

_____

2. _____

_____

3. _____

_____

4. _____

_____

5. _____

_____

Name _____ Date _____

Writing About the Big Question

What is important to know?

Big Question Vocabulary

concept	distinguish	examine	guess	judge
knowledge	limit	measure	narrow	observe
purpose	question	refer	source	study

A. *Use one or more words from the list above to complete each set of related words.*

1. conclude, answer, decide, _____

2. inspect, analyze, search, _____

3. decrease, restrict, lessen, _____

4. watch, see, look, _____

B. *Follow the directions. Write your responses in complete sentences. Use at least two words from the list above.*

1. Describe a piece of writing that you have done. What was its **purpose**? _____

_____

_____

2. How did you achieve your purpose, and what **knowledge** helped you do that?

_____

_____

_____

_____

C. *Complete the sentence below. Then, explain why such knowledge would be important to learn before the move.*

Before a family moves to a new neighborhood, family members might **question** people who already live there about _____

_____

_____

_____

_____

Name _____ Date _____

"**Langston Terrace**" by Eloise Greenfield
Reading: Identify Key Details to Determine the Main Idea

The **main idea** is the most important point in a literary work or passage. Sometimes the author states the main idea directly. Other times you can figure out the main idea by **identifying key details** in the text. Asking the following three questions can help you find the key details.

- What is this literary work about?
- What details are repeated throughout the selection?
- What details are related to other details in the selection?

For example, an essay about moving to a house in a new neighborhood might include details about why the move is necessary, how the neighborhood looks, and what the new house is like. The key details might point to a main idea of *The new neighborhood is friendly* or *We found a home at last.* Note that not every paragraph will contain a key detail. To help you find the key details, ask the three questions listed above.

DIRECTIONS: *Use this organizer to record key details as you read "Langston Terrace." The details will help you determine the main idea. The first key detail is done for you.*

1. Key detail
I fell in love with Langston Terrace the very first time I saw it.

2. Key detail

3. Key detail

4. Key detail

5. Main idea

"Langston Terrace" by Eloise Greenfield
Literary Analysis: Author's Influences

An **author's influences** are the cultural and historical factors that affect his or her writing. These factors may include the time and place of an author's birth, the author's cultural background, or world events that happened during the author's lifetime. For example, the Great Depression, which lasted through much of the 1930s, might have influenced the ideas of an author who grew up at that time. As you read, look for details that indicate an author's influences.

DIRECTIONS: *Two of the cultural and historical factors that may have influenced Eloise Greenfield are listed below. Read the information about each possible influence and answer the questions that follow.*

1. **Growing up during the Great Depression**

Eloise Greenfield was born in 1929 at the beginning of the Great Depression. The years 1929–1940 were a period of financial hardship for many people in the United States. Businesses and banks closed. People lost their jobs, their savings, and their houses. They stood in long lines waiting to get bread. Many were homeless and starving. The Great Depression affected many people, especially racial minorities who were "last hired, first fired."

A. Write one detail from the information above that tells you that the Greenfield family had little money.

_____

B. Now think about the selection "Langston Terrace." How do you think the event of the Great Depression influenced Greenfield's writing?

_____

_____

2. **Growing up in a working-class African American family**

Greenfield was the oldest of five children in a close family with many relatives. Both of her parents were high school graduates who had grown up in the South. For many years, Greenfield went back to the South every summer to visit family members there. Like most African Americans at that time, Greenfield attended segregated schools and lived in segregated housing at Langston Terrace. She graduated from high school right after the end of World War II.

A. Write one detail from the information above that tells you something about Greenfield's family.

_____

B. Think again about the selection "Langston Terrace." How do you think the time and place of Greenfield's childhood influenced her writing?

_____

_____

"Langston Terrace" by Eloise Greenfield
Vocabulary Builder

Word List

applications   choral   community   homey   resident   reunion

A. DIRECTIONS: *Circle the letter of the word or phrase that is closest in meaning to the word in CAPITAL LETTERS.*

1. APPLICATIONS:
   A. jobs
   B. requests
   C. tools
   D. methods

2. REUNION:
   A. memory
   B. labor
   C. division
   D. get-together

3. COMMUNITY:
   A. resort
   B. courage
   C. city
   D. happiness

4. CHORAL:
   A. singing
   B. dancing
   C. reading
   D. artistic

5. HOMEY:
   A. ugly
   B. beautiful
   C. modern
   D. cozy

6. RESIDENT:
   A. member
   B. manager
   C. inhabitant
   D. officer

B. WORD STUDY: *The suffix -ent can form an adjective. It means "has," "shows," or "does." Use the context of the sentence and what you know about the suffix -ent to answer each question.*

1. The coach told me I'd pitch in tomorrow's baseball game. "You're a great pitcher," he said. "I'm *confident* that you'll do a great job." What did he mean?

   _____

2. If a building catches on fire, is there an *urgent* need to call for help? Explain your answer.

   _____

3. Is getting a perfect score on a test *dependent* upon having all the answers correct? Explain.

   _____

"**Langston Terrace**" by Eloise Greenfield
Conventions: Simple Tenses of Verbs

A **verb** is a word that expresses an action or a state of being. A **verb tense** shows the time of the action or state of being. The **simple verb tenses** show present, past, and future time. Form the past tense of regular verbs with *-ed* or *-d.* Memorize the past tense of irregular verbs. Form the future tense of all verbs with the helping verb *will.*

Tenses	Regular Verb: Ask	Irregular Verb: Eat	Irregular Verb: Be
Present	I ask.	I eat.	I am.
Past	I asked.	I ate.	I was.
Future	I will ask.	I will eat.	I will be.

A. PRACTICE: *Underline the verb in each sentence. Then, on the line before the sentence, write whether the verb is in the* present, past, *or* future *tense.*

_____ 1. We will move soon to a new neighborhood.

_____ 2. We placed our belongings in boxes a couple of days ago.

_____ 3. Builders chose a hilltop as the site for our neighborhood.

_____ 4. Our new home looks beautiful.

_____ 5. We will make new friends at a new school.

_____ 6. I liked our old neighborhood.

_____ 7. Last May, my parents first thought about moving.

_____ 8. I am sad about this move from our old house.

B. Writing Application: *Write a sentence about your neighborhood, using one or more verbs in the past tense. Then, rewrite the sentence using verbs in the present tense. Finally, rewrite the sentence using verbs in the future tense. Study these examples:*

PAST TENSE: Neighborhood children <u>played</u> lots of games in the park and <u>grew</u> tired at the end of the day.

PRESENT TENSE: My brother still <u>plays</u> in the park, but he <u>grows</u> tired less often.

FUTURE: Next year he <u>will play</u> on the baseball team, but he probably <u>will grow</u> tired of sitting on the bench.

_____

_____

_____

_____

_____

"Langston Terrace" by Eloise Greenfield
Support for Writing to Sources: Journal Entry

For your journal entry, first decide on the event from the essay about which you want to write. Then, use the graphic organizer below to jot down words and phrases that describe "your" (Greenfield's) thoughts and feelings about the event.

The event: _____

I feel		I think

How You (as Greenfield) React to the Event

I feel		I think

Use your notes to write a journal entry that describes the event and your reaction as Eloise Greenfield. Remember to write from her point of view.

All-in-One Workbook
83

"Langston Terrace" by Eloise Greenfield

Support for Research and Technology: Informative Presentation

With a small group, prepare an informative presentation on the importance of community. Use library resources and reputable online sources to research your topic. Use the chart below to take notes on the information you find.

Ways in Which the Community Is Important

Now, prepare a poster to present your findings. Use images or photographs from magazines or the Internet to illustrate your ideas.

Name _____ Date _____

from **The Pigman & Me** by Paul Zindel
Writing About the Big Question
What is important to know?

Big Question Vocabulary

concept	distinguish	examine	guess	judge
knowledge	limit	measure	narrow	observe
purpose	question	refer	source	study

A. *Give an example of each of the following.*

1. A **concept** about our planet: _____

2. A reliable Internet research **source**: _____

3. A device used to **measure**: _____

4. Something that you often **observe** on your way to school: _____

B. *Answer the questions. Write your responses in complete sentences. Use at least two words from the list above.*

1. What steps do you follow to study for a social studies or science test?

   _____

   _____

   _____

   _____

2. How do these steps help you remember the facts you need to complete the test well?

   _____

   _____

   _____

   _____

C. *Complete the sentence below. Then, suggest a new rule that you would put in place at school if you were the principal.*

The **purpose** of having rules at school is _____

_____

_____

_____

_____

Name _____   Date _____

from **The Pigman & Me** by Paul Zindel
Reading: Determine Main Idea by Distinguishing Between Important and Unimportant Details

The **main idea** is the most important point in a literary work. Individual paragraphs or sections may also have a central idea that supports the main idea of the work. To determine the main idea, look at details in the story and **distinguish between important and unimportant details.** Important details are also called supporting details. They are minor pieces of information that tell more about the main idea.

- Ask yourself questions about details in a literary work. For example: *Why did the author include this detail? Does this detail help readers better understand the main idea?*
- Keep in mind that not all details support the main idea.

DIRECTIONS: *Read the example from* The Pigman & Me. *The important details, those that have something to do with trouble that is about to happen, have been underlined.*

Example: <u>When trouble came to me, it didn't involve anybody I thought it would. It involved the nice, normal, smart boy by the name of John Quinn.</u> Life does that to us a lot. Just when we think something awful's going to happen one way, it throws you a curve and the something awful happens another way.

Now read passages 1 and 2 below, and underline the details that seem important to you. Then, complete the chart that follows the passages.

1. What I didn't know was that you were allowed to sign out the paddles for only fifteen minutes per period so more kids could get a chance to use them. I just didn't happen to know that little rule, and Richard Cahill didn't think to tell me about it. Richard was getting a drink from the water fountain when John Quinn came up to me and told me I had to give him my paddle.

2. That was when I did something berserk. I was so wound up and frightened that I didn't think, and I struck out at him with my right fist. I had forgotten I was holding the paddle, and it smacked into his face, giving him an instant black eye. John was shocked. I was shocked. Richard Cahill came running back to me and he was shocked.

	One Important Detail	**One Unimportant Detail**
Example	It involved the nice, normal, smart boy by the name of John Quinn.	Life does that to us a lot.
Passage 1		
Passage 2		

What is the main idea of the two passages from *The Pigman & Me?* _____

_____

Name _____ Date _____

from **The Pigman & Me** by Paul Zindel
Literary Analysis: Mood

Mood is the overall feeling a literary work produces in a reader. For example, the mood of a work may be happy, sad, scary, or hopeful. To create a particular mood, writers carefully choose words and create word pictures that appeal to the senses.

Some literary works present a single mood throughout a selection. In other works, the mood may change as the piece progresses.

A. DIRECTIONS: *Read the following passages, and circle the words, phrases, or details that help create a certain mood for the reader. On the line below each passage, write a sentence to describe the mood.*

1. That was all he had to say, and I spilled out each and every horrifying detail. Nonno Frankie let me babble on and on. He looked as if he understood exactly how I felt and wasn't going to call me stupid or demented or a big yellow coward. When I didn't have another word left in me, I just shut up and stared down at the ground.

   Mood: _____

2. "Yes, you curse this John Quinn. You tell him, 'May your left ear wither and fall into your right pocket!' And you tell him he looks like a fugitive from a brain gang! And tell him he has a face like a mattress! And that an espresso coffee cup would fit on his head like a sombrero. And then you just give him the big Sicilian surprise!"

   Mood: _____

B. Directions: *Use the organizer below to record other details in* The Pigman & Me *that help to create a mood. Use the space in the center to name the mood or feeling you get when you read the selection. Then, jot down three details that contribute to this mood.*

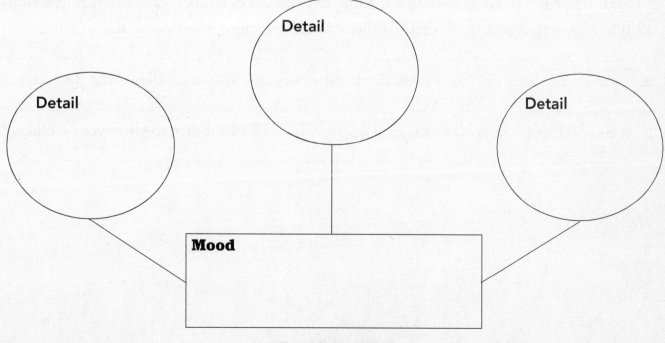

Name _____   Date _____

from **The Pigman & Me** by Paul Zindel
Vocabulary Builder

Word List

condemnation   demented   distorted   exact   observant   undulating

A. DIRECTIONS: *Use a dictionary or a thesaurus to help you find a* **synonym,** *a word that means the same or nearly the same, for each vocabulary word. Then, use each vocabulary word in a sentence that makes the meaning of the word clear.*

Example: berserk   synonym: crazy

Sentence: Berserk with anger, the bear fought off the attack on her cub.

1. **exact** (used as a verb)   synonym: _____

   Sentence: _____

2. **undulating**   synonym: _____

   Sentence: _____

3. **demented**   synonym: _____

   Sentence: _____

4. **observant**   synonym: _____

   Sentence: _____

5. **condemnation**   synonym: _____

   Sentence: _____

6. **distorted** (used as an adjective)   synonym: _____

   Sentence: _____

B. WORD STUDY: The Latin root *-tort-* means "to twist out of shape." Answer each question.

1. When a snake coils up to rest, it is in a *tortile* position. What does that word mean?

   _____

2. *Tortellini* are pieces of pasta twisted into little pouches. Why were they given that name?

   _____

3. If you suddenly got good news, how might you *contort* your face to show your feelings?

   _____

All-in-One Workbook
88

Name _____ Date _____

Conventions: Perfect Tenses of Verbs

The **perfect tenses** of verbs combine a form of the helping verb *have* with the past participle of the main verb. The past participle usually ends in *-ed* or *-d*.

- The **present perfect tense** shows an action that began in the past and continues into the present.
- The **past perfect tense** shows a past action or condition that ended before another past action began.
- The **future perfect tense** shows a future action or condition that will have ended before another begins.

Present Perfect	Past Perfect	Future Perfect
have, has + past participle	had + past participle	will have + past participle
They *have arrived.*	They *had arrived* before we came.	They *will have arrived* before the show starts.

A. PRACTICE: *Complete each sentence by using the form of the verb requested in parentheses. Write the verb on the line provided.*

(receive-past perfect)   **1.** By the time we arrived, the winners _____ their awards.

(remain-present perfect) **2.** Even though we are in a tough situation, Morgan

_____ calm.

(learn-future perfect)   **3.** Before the year ends, I _____ to defend myself.

(try-present perfect)   **4.** The candidate _____ to explain, but the voters still

don't believe her.

(score-past perfect)   **5.** By the time the game ended, Ollie _____ three goals.

(heal-future perfect)   **6.** When we see Lee again, his bruises _____ .

B. Writing Application: *Write a paragraph about a time when you were misunderstood. Use verbs in the present perfect, past perfect, and future perfect tenses. Use each of the three perfect tenses at least once.*

_____

_____

_____

_____

_____

_____

Name _____   Date _____

from **The Pigman & Me** by Paul Zindel

Support for Writing to Sources: Problem-and-Solution Essay

Use the following chart to write your problem-and-solution essay to help a newcomer adjust to a new school. Write a problem that the newcomer might face on the line provided. Then, list the possible solutions in the chart. Include evidence to support each solution.

Problem: _____

_____

Solutions to the Problem

from **The Pigman & Me** by Paul Zindel
Support for Speaking and Listening: Informal Discussion

Use the chart below or make your own chart on a separate sheet of paper to take notes during your informal discussion. Then, use your notes to help you summarize the group's ideas about how new students should act in order to make friends.

Actions New Students Should Take	Actions New Students Should Avoid Taking
_____	_____
_____	_____
_____	_____
_____	_____
_____	_____
_____	_____
_____	_____
_____	_____
_____	_____
_____	_____
_____	_____
_____	_____
_____	_____
_____	_____
_____	_____
_____	_____

Summary: _____

_____

_____

"The Seven Wonders of the World" and **"Art, Architecture, and Learning in Egypt"**

Writing About the Big Question

What is important to know?

Big Question Vocabulary

concept	distinguish	examine	guess	judge
knowledge	limit	measure	narrow	observe
purpose	question	refer	source	study

A. *Write down one or more words from the list above that help describe how you might learn each piece of information.*

1. the length of a line _____

2. the best CD player to buy _____

3. how birds build nests _____

4. the scientist who discovered penicillin _____

B. *Answer each question in full sentences. Include at least two words from the list above.*

1. What is the most effective way to gather facts for a research report?

   _____

   _____

   _____

2. What could a person do to learn about important issues in his or her community?

   _____

   _____

   _____

C. *Complete the sentence below. Then, write a short paragraph in which you connect your point of view to the Big Question, telling how people can increase their knowledge through careful communication skills.*

To communicate with others clearly, it is important to _____

_____

_____

_____

_____

_____

"The Seven Wonders of the World" and "Art, Architecture, and Learning in Egypt"
Reading: Use Text Aids and Features

Informational texts often use **text aids and features** to convey central ideas, highlight important information, and help the reader see relationships among ideas in a text. As you read "The Seven Wonders of the World" and "Art, Architecture, and Learning in Egypt," use the chart below to identify the **text aids** and **text features** in each selection. Then, answer the questions that follow.

Text Aids and Text Features	
Examples from "The Seven Wonders of the World"	**Examples from "Art, Architecture, and Learning in Egypt"**
_____	_____
_____	_____
_____	_____
_____	_____
_____	_____
_____	_____
_____	_____
_____	_____
_____	_____
_____	_____
_____	_____
_____	_____

Now, review your notes in the chart above, and answer the following questions.

1. Which type of text aid or feature did you find more helpful? _____

2. In your opinion, which of these two selections has more useful text aids and features? Explain.

_____

_____

3. What other text aids and features would you like to have included in informational texts such as these two?

_____

_____

All-in-One Workbook
93

"The Seven Wonders of the World" and "Art, Architecture, and Learning in Egypt"
Vocabulary Builder

Word List

   archaeologists   architect   colossal

A. PRACTICE: *Write a sentence using each of the listed vocabulary words. Then, apply your knowledge by writing another sentence, using a different form of each word, as indicated.*

1. **a. archaeologists** _____

   _____

   b. archaeological *adj.* related to the study of past human life and culture _____

   _____

   _____

2. **a. architect** _____

   _____

   b. architecture *n.* the manner or style in which something is built _____

   _____

   _____

3. **a. colossal** _____

   _____

   b. colossus *n.* a person or a thing that is huge in size or power _____

   _____

   _____

B. WRITING APPLICATION: *Write a brief paragraph about one of the Seven Wonders of the World. Use each of the vocabulary words at least once in your paragraph.*

_____

_____

_____

_____

_____

_____

_____

Name _____ Date _____

"The Seven Wonders of the World" and "Art, Architecture, and Learning in Egypt"
Support for Writing to Compare Expository Texts

Use the chart below to collect information about text aids or structural features that you find in an online almanac and a textbook. Describe each feature in column one. Then put a check mark in the column which indicates where the feature appears.

	Online Almanac	**Textbook**
Feature: _____ _____ _____ _____ _____		
Feature: _____ _____ _____ _____ _____		
Feature: _____ _____ _____ _____ _____		

On the lines below, record your findings.

1. Features found in online almanac only: _____

   _____

2. Features found in textbook only: _____

   _____

3. Features found in both sources: _____

   _____

Writing Process
Comparison-and-Contrast Essay

Prewriting: Gathering Details

Use the following Venn diagram to gather facts, descriptions, and examples that you can use to make comparisons and contrasts. Record details in the outside sections about how each subject is different. Use the overlapping middle section to record details about how the subjects are alike.

Subject 1: _____   Subject 2: _____

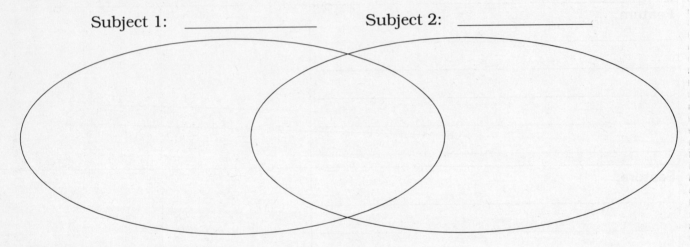

Drafting: Choosing an Organizational Pattern

Use the following graphic organizers to help you decide whether the block method or the point-by-point method is the better organizational plan for your essay.

Block Method

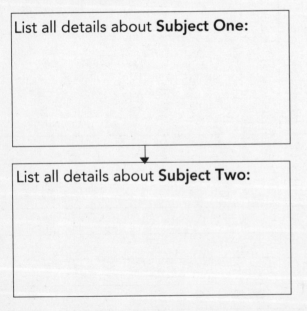

List all details about **Subject One:**

List all details about **Subject Two:**

Point-by-Point Method

Subject 1	Subject 2
First Point:	First Point:
Second Point:	Second Point:
Third Point:	Third Point:
Fourth Point:	Fourth Point:

Name _____ Date _____

Conventions: Irregular Verbs and Troublesome Verbs

In irregular verbs, the past and past participle are not formed by adding -ed or -d to the present tense. Listed below are three examples of commonly used irregular verbs.

Present	Present Participle	Past	Past Participle
begin	(am) beginning	began	(have) begun
drive	(am) driving	drove	(have) driven
go	(am) going	went	(have) gone

Troublesome verbs are verb pairs that are easily confused.

Troublesome Verb Pairs (lay/lie, raise/rise, set/sit)	Example
Lay means "to put or place something." *Lie* means "to be situated."	Tom *laid* the pen on the table. Barb *is lying* in the hammock.
Raise means "to lift up." It takes a direct object. *Rise* means "to get up." It does not take a direct object.	The wind *has raised* some dust. My neighbors *rise* very early.
Set means "to put something in a certain place." It takes a direct object. *Sit* means "to rest." It does not take a direct object.	Ms. Wendt *set* the vase near the window. Jamie *is sitting* near the pool.

A. PRACTICE: *On the line, write the letter of the correct verb for the sentence.*

1. The game _____ five minutes ago.
   A. begin   B. began   C. begun

2. The Wildcats have already _____ all the water in their bottles.
   A. drink   B. drank   C. drunk

3. We're waiting for LaRue to _____ one in for our team.
   A. lay   B. lie   C. laid

4. The crowd will _____ to cheer if we score now.
   A. raise   B. rise   C. risen

B. WRITING APPLICATION: *On the lines, rewrite the italicized words using the correct verb forms.*

1. Our team mascot *bring* his costume with him last night. _____

2. We're behind, but our team is *done* our best. _____

3. The referee will *sit* the ball down. _____

4. Look! They have *drove* the ball down the field. _____

Name _____   Date _____

"Jackie Robinson, Justice at Last" by Geoffrey Ward and Ken Burns
Vocabulary Builder

Selection Vocabulary

     integrate   prejudiced   superb

A. DIRECTIONS: *In each item below, think about the meaning of the italicized word, and then, answer the question.*

1. Parents have suggested that the middle school *integrate* its athletic teams so girls and boys will play on the same team. Is this a good idea? Why or why not?

_____

_____

2. Some students have ideas that lead them to be *prejudiced* against recycling rules. What might you say to persuade them otherwise?

_____

_____

3. Your best friend has asked you to recommend a *superb* movie. What movie would you recommend? Explain your choice.

_____

_____

Academic Vocabulary

     affect   opinions   support

B. DIRECTIONS: *On the line, write whether each statement below is TRUE or FALSE. Then, explain your answer.*

_____ 1. Weather does not *affect* the players in a baseball game.

_____

_____ 2. People have different *opinions* about what makes a great baseball player.

_____

_____ 3. Devoted baseball fans *support* their hometown teams.

_____

"Jackie Robinson, Justice at Last" by Geoffrey Ward and Ken Burns
Take Notes for Discussion

Before the Group Discussion: Read the following passage from the selection in your textbook.

> But somehow this man had to rise above that. No matter what happened, he must never lose his temper. No matter what was said to him, he must never answer back. If he had even one fight, people might say integration wouldn't work.

During the Discussion: As the group discusses each question, take notes on how other students' ideas either differ from or build upon your own.

Discussion Questions	Other Responses	Comparison to My Responses
1. Why could a single fight damage the cause of integration?		
2. In what way was Robinson's refusal to fight back a way of fighting *for* something?		

Name _____ Date _____

"Jackie Robinson, Justice at Last" by Geoffrey Ward and Ken Burns
Take Notes for Writing to Sources

Planning Your Informative Text: Before you begin drafting your **comparison-contrast essay,** use the chart below to organize your ideas.

Branch Rickey	Jackie Robinson
Obstacles to overcome:	Obstacles to overcome:
Details from Text:	Details from Text:

Name _____ Date _____

"Jackie Robinson, Justice at Last" by Geoffrey Ward and Ken Burns
Take Notes for Research

As you research **how gender segregation is still practiced in amateur and professional baseball and how some people have fought against this bias,** use the forms below to take notes from your sources. As necessary, continue your notes on the back of this page, on note cards, or in a word-processing document.

Source Information   Check one: ☐ Primary Source   ☐ Secondary Source

Title: _____   Author: _____

Publication Information: _____

Page(s): _____

Main Idea: _____

_____

Quotation or Paraphrase: _____

_____

Source Information   Check one: ☐ Primary Source   ☐ Secondary Source

Title: _____   Author: _____

Publication Information: _____

Page(s): _____

Main Idea: _____

_____

Quotation or Paraphrase: _____

_____

Source Information   Check one: ☐ Primary Source   ☐ Secondary Source

Title: _____   Author: _____

Publication Information: _____

Page(s): _____

Main Idea: _____

_____

Quotation or Paraphrase: _____

_____

"Memories of an All-American Girl" by Carmen Pauls
Vocabulary Builder

Selection Vocabulary

exhilarating   immortality   inductions

A. DIRECTIONS: *For each sentence, explain whether it makes sense based on the meaning of the italicized word. If it does not make sense, write a new sentence using the word correctly.*

1. If a baseball game is *exhilarating*, you will probably get bored.

   _____

2. If human beings enjoyed *immortality*, people would have an unlimited time to accomplish their dreams.

   _____

3. *Inductions* into the Baseball Hall of Fame are a reason for celebration.

   _____

Academic Vocabulary

reflecting   visual

B. DIRECTIONS: *Complete each sentence with a word, phrase, or clause that contains a context clue for the italicized word.*

1. *Visual* aids help you understand a complicated idea because _____

   _____

2. *Reflecting* on a difficult passage from a story is helpful because _____

   _____

"**Memories of an All-American Girl**" by Carmen Pauls
Take Notes for Discussion

Before the Partner Discussion: Read the passage from the selection in your textbook that begins and ends as shown below.

> ... [T]he girls, from what was sometimes called the "American Glamor League," ... they all looked so funny in skirts.

During the Discussion: As you discuss each question, take notes on how your partner's ideas either differ from or build upon your own.

Discussion Questions	Other Ideas Expressed	Comparison to My Own Ideas
1. How were women players treated differently from male players?		
2. Do you think the women players were treated unfairly? Why or why not?		

Name _____ Date _____

"**Memories of an All-American Girl**" by Carmen Pauls
Take Notes for Research

As you research **the history of women in baseball,** you can use the organizer below to take notes from your sources. As necessary, continue your notes on the back of this page, on note cards, or in a word-processing document.

History of Women in Baseball	
Main Idea _____ _____ Quotation or Paraphrase _____ _____ _____ _____ Source Information _____ _____ _____ _____	Main Idea _____ _____ Quotation or Paraphrase _____ _____ _____ _____ Source Information _____ _____ _____ _____
Main Idea _____ _____ Quotation or Paraphrase _____ _____ _____ _____ Source Information _____ _____ _____ _____	Main Idea _____ _____ Quotation or Paraphrase _____ _____ _____ _____ Source Information _____ _____ _____ _____

"Memories of an All-American Girl" by Carmen Pauls
Take Notes for Writing to Sources

Planning Your Autobiographical Narrative: Before you begin drafting your autobiographical narrative, use the chart below to organize your ideas.

1. Details about the opportunity or challenge you faced:

_____

_____

_____

_____

_____

2. Visual details to create vivid images for your audience:

_____

_____

_____

_____

3. Reflections on the impact of the event:

_____

_____

_____

_____

_____

_____

_____

_____

_____

_____

_____

All-in-One Workbook
105

Name _____ Date _____

"Preserving a Great American Symbol" by Richard Durbin
Vocabulary Builder

Selection Vocabulary

amendment   doomed   extinction

A. DIRECTIONS: *Write two different sentences for each vocabulary word. You may use different forms of the vocabulary word for your second sentence if you choose.*

> **Example:** She gave a <u>humorous</u> speech.
> Her <u>humor</u> was appreciated by everyone present.

1. amendment

_____

_____

2. doomed

_____

_____

3. extinction

_____

_____

Academic Vocabulary

achieve   argue   cite

B. DIRECTIONS: *Following the directions, answer each question in a complete sentence.*

1. Describe a difficult goal that an athlete might want to *achieve.*

_____

_____

2. Write a sentence in which you *argue* that Babe Ruth (or another athlete) is the greatest.

_____

_____

3. *Cite* two reasons that you like or dislike a particular sport.

_____

_____

Name _____ Date _____

Take Notes for Discussion

Before the Panel Discussion: Read the following passage from the selection.

> Please do not try to sell me on the notion that these metal clubs will make better hitters.

> What will be next? Teflon baseballs? Radar-enhanced gloves? I ask you.

During the Discussion: As the panel discusses each question, take notes on how other students' ideas either differ from or build upon your own.

Discussion Questions	Other Ideas Expressed	Comparison to My Own Ideas
1. What might be the effects of "radar-enhanced gloves"?		
2. What does Durbin imply about the effects of technology in sports? What are his reasons for making this argument?		

"Preserving a Great American Symbol" by Richard Durbin
Take Notes for Research

As you research **some of baseball's most well-known traditions and how these traditions affect players and fans today,** you can use the organizer below to take notes from your sources. As necessary, continue your notes on the back of this page, on note cards, or in a word-processing document.

Baseball Traditions

Main Idea _____

Quotation or Paraphrase _____
_____
_____
_____

Source Information _____
_____
_____
_____

Main Idea _____

Quotation or Paraphrase _____
_____
_____
_____

Source Information _____
_____
_____
_____

Main Idea _____

Quotation or Paraphrase _____
_____
_____
_____

Source Information _____
_____
_____
_____

Main Idea _____

Quotation or Paraphrase _____
_____
_____
_____

Source Information _____
_____
_____
_____

"Preserving a Great American Symbol" by Richard Durbin
Take Notes for Writing to Sources

Planning Your Argument: Before you begin drafting your **persuasive speech,** use the chart below to organize your ideas.

1. The issue and your position:

_____

_____

_____

_____

_____

_____

_____

_____

2. Logic and evidence to support your position:

_____

_____

_____

_____

_____

_____

_____

_____

3. Conclusion to appeal directly to your audience:

_____

_____

_____

_____

_____

_____

_____

_____

_____

"The Southpaw" by Judith Viorst
Vocabulary Builder

Selection Vocabulary

former   unreasonable

A. DIRECTIONS: *Write one example of people or things that demonstrate the meaning of each word. Follow this example.*

REFERENCES: encyclopedia articles

1. FORMER: _____

2. UNREASONABLE: _____

Academic Vocabulary

anticipate   conclude

B. DIRECTIONS: *Write at least one synonym, one antonym, and an example sentence for each word. Synonyms and antonyms can be words or phrases.*

Word	Synonym	Antonym	Example Sentence
anticipate			
conclude			

Name _____ Date _____

"The Southpaw" by Judith Viorst
Take Notes for Discussion

Before the Group Discussion: Read the passage from the selection in your textbook that begins and ends as shown below.

> "Dear Richard, Don't invite me to your birthday party... when you go for your checkup you need a tetanus shot."

During the Discussion: As you discuss each question, take notes on how other students' ideas either differ from or build upon your own.

Discussion Questions	Other Ideas Expressed	Comparison to My Own Ideas
1. In this quarrel, which statements are fair? Which are not?		
2. Is this disagreement worthy of breaking up a friendship? Why or why not?		

Name _____ Date _____

"The Southpaw" by Judith Viorst
Take Notes for Research

As you research **baseball's popularity around the world**, use the forms below to take notes from your sources. As necessary, continue your notes on the back of this page, on note cards, or in a word-processing document.

The Worldwide Popularity of Baseball	
Main Idea _____	Main Idea _____
Quotation or Paraphrase _____	Quotation or Paraphrase _____
Source Information _____	Source Information _____
Main Idea _____	Main Idea _____
Quotation or Paraphrase _____	Quotation or Paraphrase _____
Source Information _____	Source Information _____

"The Southpaw" by Judith Viorst
Take Notes for Writing to Sources

Planning Your Persuasive Letter: Before you begin drafting your **persuasive letter,** use the chart below to organize your ideas.

1. Facts and evidence to support your claim:

_____
_____
_____
_____
_____
_____
_____
_____
_____

2. Responses to possible arguments against your claim:

_____
_____
_____
_____
_____
_____
_____
_____
_____

3. Conclude with a summary:

_____
_____
_____
_____
_____
_____
_____
_____
_____

Name _____ Date _____

"Red Sox Get Ready to Celebrate 100 Years at Fenway"
by Larry Fine
Vocabulary Builder

Selection Vocabulary

deficit   deft   inaugural

A. DIRECTIONS: *Write the letter of the word or phrase that is the best synonym for the italicized word. Then use the italicized word in a complete sentence.*

_____ 1. *deficit*

     A. plenty   C. abundance

     B. lack   D. definition

_____

_____ 2. *deft*

     A. awkward   C. wrong or illegal

     B. silent   D. skillful

_____

_____ 3. *inaugural*

     A. first   C. well-preserved

     B. final   D. latest

_____

Academic Vocabulary

cite   position   unique

B. DIRECTIONS: *Follow the directions in each item. Write your answer as a complete sentence that uses the italicized word.*

1. Name a source that you might *cite* in a report on baseball. _____

2. Describe a quality that is *unique* to your hometown. _____

_____

3. Explain your *position* on tearing down old ballparks and replacing them with new ones.

_____

_____

"Red Sox Get Ready to Celebrate 100 Years at Fenway"
by Larry Fine
Take Notes for Discussion

Before the Group Discussion: Read the following passage from the selection.

> While the footprint of the stadium remains, Fenway has had numerous facelifts over the decades. . . . Two years later a 23½-foot tall screen was added on top of the wall to protect the windows of buildings on adjoining Lansdowne Street.

During the Discussion: As you discuss each question, take notes on how other students' ideas either differ from or build upon your own.

Discussion Questions	Other Ideas Expressed	Comparison to My Own Ideas
1. How has Fenway Park both changed and stayed the same since it opened in 1912?		
2. How do the reasons for upgrades made in the 1930s compare with the reasons for more recent upgrades?		

Name _____ Date _____

"Red Sox Get Ready to Celebrate 100 Years at Fenway"
by Larry Fine
Take Notes for Research

As you research **to identify and learn about a ballpark or sports stadium that interests you,** you can use the organizer below to take notes from your sources. As necessary, continue your notes on the back of this page, on note cards, or in a word-processing document.

Source Information Check one: ☐ Primary Source ☐ Secondary Source

Title: _____ Author: _____

Publication Information: _____

Page(s): _____

Main Idea: _____

_____

Quotation or Paraphrase: _____

_____

Source Information Check one: ☐ Primary Source ☐ Secondary Source

Title: _____ Author: _____

Publication Information: _____

Page(s): _____

Main Idea: _____

_____

Quotation or Paraphrase: _____

_____

Source Information Check one: ☐ Primary Source ☐ Secondary Source

Title: _____ Author: _____

Publication Information: _____

Page(s): _____

Main Idea: _____

_____

Quotation or Paraphrase: _____

_____

Name _____ Date _____

"Red Sox Get Ready to Celebrate 100 Years at Fenway"
by Larry Fine
Take Notes for Writing to Sources

Planning Your Argument: Before you begin drafting your **argument,** use the chart below to organize your ideas.

1. Notes about Fenway Park for your introduction:

_____
_____
_____
_____
_____

2. The issue and your position:

_____
_____
_____
_____
_____

3. Your claim with evidence from the text:

_____
_____
_____
_____
_____

4. Notes for your conclusion:

_____
_____
_____
_____
_____

Name _____ Date _____

"Why We Love Baseball" by Mark Newman
Vocabulary Builder

Selection Vocabulary

diversion   premise   ventured

A. DIRECTIONS: *Write an explanation for your answer to each question.*

1. When someone tells you that going to a baseball game is a great *diversion,* how would you answer?

   _____

2. If a friend tells you that he or she has *ventured* into skydiving, what advice would you give?

   _____

3. Do you agree with the *premise* that playing a sport builds character?

   _____

Academic Vocabulary

facts   research   sources

B. DIRECTIONS: *Complete each sentence with a word, phrase, or clause that contains a context clue for the italicized word.*

1. Listing the *sources* for a report is important because _____

   _____.

2. One way to organize information for a *research* project is to _____

   _____.

3. Including *facts* to support an argument is helpful because _____

   _____.

"Why We Love Baseball" by Mark Newman
Take Notes for Discussion

Before the Group Discussion: Read the passage from the selection in your textbook that begins and ends as show below.

The game gets inside you … as far back as I can remember.

During the Discussion: As you discuss each question, take notes on how other students' ideas either differ from or build upon your own.

Discussion Questions	Other Ideas Expressed	Comparison to My Own Ideas
1. What does Wedge mean by "The game gets inside you"?		
2. Does Wedge's argument appeal to emotion or to reason? Which do you think makes a stronger argument? Why?		

"Why We Love Baseball" by Mark Newman

Take Notes for Research

As you research **different literary forms about baseball,** you can use the organizer below to take notes from your sources. Under "Source Information," be sure to include each selection's publisher and date of publication. As necessary, continue your notes on the back of this page, on note cards, or in a word-processing document.

Poems, Novels, Memoirs, and Essays About Baseball	
Title and Author _____ _____ Summary _____ _____ _____ _____ Source Information _____ _____ _____ _____	Title and Author _____ _____ Summary _____ _____ _____ _____ Source Information _____ _____ _____ _____
Title and Author _____ _____ Summary _____ _____ _____ _____ Source Information _____ _____ _____ _____	Title and Author _____ _____ Summary _____ _____ _____ _____ Source Information _____ _____ _____ _____

Name _____ Date _____

"Why We Love Baseball" by Mark Newman
Take Notes for Writing to Sources

Planning Your Reflective Essay: Before you begin drafting your **reflective essay,** use the chart below to organize your ideas.

---

1. Notes for your introduction to the activity:

_____

_____

_____

---

2. Reasons for liking the activity:

_____

_____

_____

_____

_____

_____

_____

---

3. Some transitional words and phrases to help you move smoothly from point to point:

_____

_____

_____

_____

---

4. Notes for your conclusion:

_____

_____

_____

_____

_____

from **Ted Williams Baseball Card**
Vocabulary Builder and Take Notes for Writing to Sources

Academic Vocabulary

contrast   reveal

A. DIRECTIONS: *Following the directions, answer each question in a complete sentence.*

1. Explain one important *contrast* between baseball and football.

_____

2. How might a baseball fan *reveal* his or her love for the sport?

_____

Take Notes for Writing to Sources

Planning Your Narrative: Before you begin drafting your **journal entry,** use the chart below to organize your ideas. First, identify the character whose point of view you will use.

CHARACTER: _____
1. Notes about the setting, characters, and events: _____ _____ _____ _____
2. Sensory and concrete details to enrich your descriptions: _____ _____ _____
3. Notes for your conclusion: _____ _____ _____

Name _____ Date _____

Unit 3: Poetry
Big Question Vocabulary—1

The Big Question: Do we need words to communicate well?

One of the main ways in which people exchange information is by using words. Words can be a clear way of telling others what is on your mind.

communicate: to exchange information with people using words, signs, or writing

dialogue: a conversation or a discussion between two or more people

language: a system of communication by written or spoken words that is used by the people of a particular country or area

quote: to repeat exactly what someone said or wrote

verbal: words spoken rather than written

DIRECTIONS: Answer the questions using the number of vocabulary words specified. You can use words more than once, but you must use all five vocabulary words.

"Use your own words!" Rosa shouted at Phil. He insisted on always copying the words of others. How was Rosa supposed to know what Phil was really thinking if they couldn't have a real conversation?

1. What problem is Rosa having with her friend Phil? Use at least two of the vocabulary words in your answer.

_____

_____

_____

"Don't shout at me and walk away," Phil responded. "Let's talk about this!"

2. What was Phil suggesting? Use at least one vocabulary word in your answer.

_____

_____

Rosa sat across the table from Phil. She began speaking. She told him that he should have confidence in his ability to express himself in words. Phil listened and agreed to speak his mind instead of hiding behind the words of others.

3. What did Phil agree to do? Use at least two vocabulary words in your answer.

_____

_____

_____

Name _____ Date _____

Unit 3: Poetry
Big Question Vocabulary—2

The Big Question: Do we need words to communicate well?

Communication between people takes place in many ways that do not involve words or speaking. Although we may not be aware of it, we are reading and interpreting signals from people all through the day.

expression: a look on someone's face or what someone writes, says, or does that shows you what he or she feels or thinks

gesture: *n.* a movement of a person's arms, hands, or head that shows what he or she means or feels; *v.* to move your arms, hands, or head to tell someone something

nonverbal: not involving words

symbolize: to represent something

visual: able to be seen

DIRECTIONS: Finish the following story in the first person. Use your imagination and all five vocabulary words listed above.

> You wake up extra late on a Saturday morning and stretch luxuriously in your bed. You have a day of fun ahead of you. You are planning to go bowling with your friends and then go to the best pizza place in town for a slice. First, you will have to talk to your parents about your plans and ask them for a ride to the bowling alley. But that should be no problem. You hear your whole family talking and having breakfast. You get up, get dressed, and brush your teeth, and then you join your family at the breakfast table. "Good morning," your Dad says cheerily. You grin and open your mouth to answer, but nothing happens. No sound comes out. You try again. Still no sound. What is wrong with you? And, more important, how are you going to ask your parents about your plans?

_____

_____

_____

_____

_____

_____

_____

_____

Unit 3: Poetry
Big Question Vocabulary—3

The Big Question: Do we need words to communicate well?

People become friends and feel close when they trust one another enough to share secrets. The communication that happens between people who are close is a special kind of communication.

connection: a situation in which two people understand and like each other

correspond: to communicate by letter

message: a spoken or written piece of information that you send to another person

reveal: to make a secret known

share: to tell others about an idea or a problem

DIRECTIONS: Think about someone with whom you are very close. It could be a friend or a family member. Put the person's name in the center circle. Then, in the surrounding ovals, answer the questions about the ways you communicate with the person.

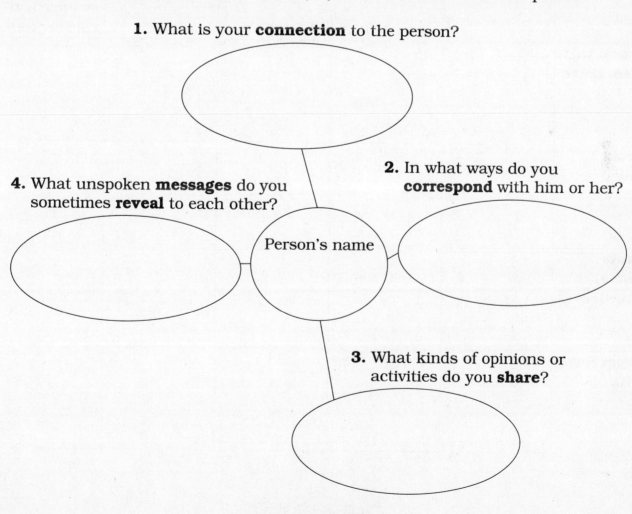

1. What is your **connection** to the person?

4. What unspoken **messages** do you sometimes **reveal** to each other?

Person's name

2. In what ways do you **correspond** with him or her?

3. What kinds of opinions or activities do you **share**?

Name _____ Date _____

Unit 3: Poetry
Applying the Big Question

Do we need words to communicate well?

DIRECTIONS: *Complete the chart below to apply what you have learned about types of communication. One row has been completed for you.*

Example	Type of information	How it is communicated	Main idea	Another way to communicate this	What I learned
From Literature	Poem: "Life Doesn't Frighten Me"	by words on a page	A person is strong and confident.	through proud facial expression or with hands on hips	Words are not always needed to show a person's strength and confidence.
From Literature					
From Science					
From Social Studies					
From Real Life					

Poetry Collection 1

Edgar Allan Poe, Maya Angelou, Lewis Carroll, Ogden Nash

Writing About the Big Question

Do we need words to communicate well?

Big Question Vocabulary

communicate   connection   correspond   dialogue   expression
gesture   language   message   nonverbal   quote
reveal   share   symbolize   verbal   visual

A. *Write a word from the list above to complete each sentence.*

1. In poems, objects can _____ ideas.

2. The _____ between objects and ideas can be a challenge to figure out.

3. Often, poetic _____ is different from everyday speech.

4. Poems can _____ important truths about life.

B. *Follow the directions in responding to each of the items below.*

1. Describe a time when you used an **expression**, **gesture**, or another form of **nonverbal communication** to **share** an opinion.

   _____

   _____

2. Write two sentences about the effect of your expression or gesture. Use at least two Big Question vocabulary words.

   _____

   _____

C. *Complete the sentence below. Then, write a short paragraph in which you connect this idea to the Big Question.*

Sometimes people fail to use language to state their real thoughts and feelings because _____

_____

_____

_____

_____

_____

Poetry Collection 1: Edgar Allan Poe, Maya Angelou, Lewis Carroll, Ogden Nash
Reading: Context Clues

When you come across a word you do not know or a word used in an unusual way, you can sometimes figure out the meaning by using context clues. **Context clues** are found in the words, phrases, and sentences surrounding an unfamiliar word. They may be words that have the same meaning or that describe or explain the word. To use context clues, **ask questions** such as these:

- *What kind of word is it?*
- *What word can I use in place of it?*
- *Which other words in the sentence explain it?*

DIRECTIONS: *Use this chart to figure out the meaning of some words that you may not know or that are used in an unusual way in the poems in this collection. For each item, write the question you would ask to figure out the meaning of the underlined word or words. Then, answer the question. Finally, write the meaning of the word or expression. The first item has been done for you.*

Word in Context	Question	Answer	Meaning
1. <u>Panthers</u> in the park / Strangers in the dark / No, they don't frighten me at all.	What kind of word is it?	It is a word that names an animal that frightens people.	kind of scary animal
2. Thus much let me <u>avow</u>— / You are not wrong			
3. I hold . . . / Grains of the golden sand— / How few! yet how they creep / Through my fingers to the <u>deep</u>			
4. The sun was shining on the sea, / . . . He did his very best to make / The <u>billows</u> smooth and bright			
5. How do, Isabel, now I'll eat you! / Isabel, Isabel, didn't worry, / Isabel didn't scream or <u>scurry</u>. / She washed her hands and she straightened her hair up, / Then Isabel quietly ate the bear up.			

Poetry Collection 1: Edgar Allan Poe, Maya Angelou, Lewis Carroll, Ogden Nash
Literary Analysis: Rhythm and Rhyme

Poets often use **rhythm** and **rhyme** to add a musical quality to their poems. **Rhythm** is the sound pattern created by stressed and unstressed syllables. Stressed syllables receive more emphasis than unstressed syllables. In this example, capital letters indicate the stressed syllables:)

    The WAL-rus AND the CAR-pen-TER (4 stressed syllables, 4 unstressed syllables)

    Were WALK-ing CLOSE at HAND (3 stressed syllables, 3 unstressed syllables)

    Rhyme is the repetition of sounds at the ends of words, such as *wall* and *hall*. Once a rhyme pattern, or rhyme scheme, has been established, you come to expect the upcoming rhymes. Many traditional poems have rhyming words at the ends of lines.

DIRECTIONS: *Rewrite each of the following lines from the poems to show their rhythm and rhyme. Write each syllable separately, as in the example above. Use capital letters to show stressed syllables. Then, circle the words that rhyme.*

1. Don't show me frogs and snakes / And listen for my scream, /
   If I'm afraid at all / It's only in my dreams.

   _____

   _____

   _____

2. *All* that we see or seem / Is but a dream within a dream.

   _____

   _____

3. "The time has come," the Walrus said, / "To talk of many things: /
   Of shoes—and ships—and sealing wax— / Of cabbages—and kings—"

   _____

   _____

   _____

4. Isabel met an enormous bear, / Isabel, Isabel, didn't care; / The bear was hungry,
   the bear was ravenous, / The bear's big mouth was cruel and cavernous.

   _____

   _____

   _____

   _____

Name _____ Date _____

Poetry Collection 1: Edgar Allan Poe, Maya Angelou, Lewis Carroll, Ogden Nash
Vocabulary Builder

Word List

beseech   cavernous   deem   dismal   ravenous   sympathize

A. DIRECTIONS: *Write the word from the Word List that best completes each sentence.*

1. My neighbor, a poet, said she would _____ her barking dogs to be quiet.

2. When the tree fell on our house, the result was a _____ hole in our roof.

3. The editors will surely _____ the excellent poem worthy of publication.

4. I _____ with my friend who lost her dog.

5. After her adventure, Isabel was _____.

6. After five days of _____ weather, we were ready for a sunny day.

B. WORD STUDY: *The root* -mal- *means "bad" or "evil." Answer each of the following questions using one of these words containing* -mal-: *dismal, malady, malfunction, malice, malign.*

1. What do you do if there is a *malfunction* of your computer?

_____

2. If someone bears you *malice*, how does that person treat you?

_____

3. What would be the normal reaction to a *dismal* story?

_____

4. How would someone feel after a long *malady*?

_____

5. What might someone do to *malign* an honest person?

_____

Name _____ Date _____

Conventions: Adjectives and Adverbs

An **adjective** modifies or describes a noun or pronoun. An **adverb** modifies a verb, an adjective, or another adverb.

Adjectives answer the questions *What kind? Which one? How many?* and *How much?* Adverbs answer the questions *How? When? Where?* and *To what extent?* Many adverbs end in *-ly.*

Example	Adjective or Adverb	Word It Modifies
We waited <u>patiently</u>.	*patiently:* adverb	*waited* (verb)
The train is <u>fast</u>.	*fast:* adjective	*train* (noun)
They are <u>tired</u>.	*tired:* adjective	*They* (pronoun)
The paintings are <u>very</u> beautiful.	*very:* adverb	*beautiful* (adjective)
Time passed <u>too</u> quickly.	*too:* adverb	*quickly* (adverb)

A. PRACTICE: *On the line provided, write whether the underlined word in each sentence is an adverb or adjective. Then, circle the word that the underlined word modifies.*

_____ 1. Paul <u>accidentally</u> forgot his best friend's birthday.

_____ 2. At the end of the day, we were <u>quite</u> tired.

_____ 3. We were extremely <u>disappointed</u> when the show was canceled.

_____ 4. The jugglers are planning an <u>exciting</u> routine.

_____ 5. He <u>patiently</u> taught the children how to read and write.

_____ 6. The lawyer is sometimes <u>almost</u> too clever.

B. Writing Application: *Describe something that happened at school. Use at least three adjectives and three adverbs in your description.*

_____

_____

_____

_____

_____

_____

_____

_____

_____

_____

Name _____ Date _____

Poetry Collection 1: Ogden Nash, Edgar Allan Poe, Maya Angelou, Lewis Carroll
Support for Writing to Sources: Letter to an Author

Use this form to draft a **letter to the author** of one of the poems in this collection. Be sure to state your reaction to the poem and tell whether or not you like the poem. Include reasons for your reaction, and refer to the poem to support your reasons.

Heading: Your address and the date _____

_____

_____

_____

Inside Address: Where the letter will be sent _____

_____

_____

Greeting Dear _____,

Begin the **body** of the letter. *State your overall reaction.* _____

_____

_____

State reasons for your reaction, and give examples to support reasons. _____

_____

_____

_____

_____

_____

_____

_____

Closing and **Signature** _____

_____

Now, write a final draft of your letter to the author of one of the poems in this collection.

Poetry Collection 1: Ogden Nash, Edgar Allan Poe, Maya Angelou, Lewis Carroll

Support for Research and Technology: Booklet

For this assignment, you will use the Internet and other sources to gather a variety of poems and illustrations to include in a booklet about facing fears. Include the poem "Life Doesn't Frighten Me" as well as other poems you enjoy. Then, organize those materials in a **booklet**. Use this chart to draft your booklet's annotations—the descriptive comments about each poem.

Poem	Annotation	
	Message About Facing Fears	**Language and Literary Devices**

Poetry Collection 2

Sandra Cisneros, Nikki Giovanni, Langston Hughes, and Emily Dickinson

Writing About the Big Question

Do we need words to communicate well?

Big Question Vocabulary

communicate	connection	correspond	dialogue	expression
gesture	language	message	nonverbal	quote
reveal	share	symbolize	verbal	visual

A. *Write one or more words from the list above to complete each sentence.*

1. I sent a text _____ to my best friend.

2. Two or more people can have a _____.

3. The tone of someone's voice should _____ with his or her feelings.

4. A crossword puzzle requires both _____ and _____ skills.

B. *Follow the directions in responding to each of the items below.*

1. Describe a situation in which you **communicated** your feelings of love or friendship in an unusual way.

   _____

   _____

2. Write two sentences that describe the reaction of the person who received your unusual communication. Use at least two Big Question vocabulary words.

   _____

   _____

C. *Complete the sentence below. Then, write a short paragraph in which you connect this idea to the Big Question.*

The way I communicate my love to the people close to me is _____

_____

_____

_____

_____

_____

Name _____ Date _____

Poetry Collection 2: Sandra Cisneros, Nikki Giovanni, Langston Hughes, Emily Dickinson
Reading: Reread and Read Ahead to Find Context Clues

Context is the situation in which a word or an expression is used. The words and phrases in the surrounding text give you clues to the meaning of the word. Sometimes a word has more than one meaning. You may recognize a word but not recognize the way in which it is used. **Reread and read ahead** to find and use context clues that clarify meanings of words with multiple meanings. Look at the following examples to see how context clarifies the meaning of *flow:*

> a river would stop / its <u>flow</u> if only / a stream were there / to receive it (*Flow* is a noun that means "steady stream of water.")

> The streams <u>flow</u> into the river. (*Flow* is a verb that means "to move along steadily.")

As you read the poems, notice words that are used in unfamiliar or unusual ways. Use the context to help determine the meaning of the words.

DIRECTIONS: *Study the underlined word in each of the following lines from "Abuelito Who" or "April Rain Song." Look for context clues in the lines that hint at the meaning of the word. On the line, write the context clues. Then, write two meanings for the word— first the meaning that fits the context and then a meaning that does* not *fit the context. The first item has been done for you.*

1. "who is a <u>watch</u> and glass of water"

   Context clues: <u>"glass of water" (something put on a table next to a bed)</u>

   Meaning in context: <u>small device for telling time</u> **Second meaning:** <u>to look at</u>

2. "Who tells me in Spanish you are my <u>diamond</u> / who tells me in English you are my sky"

   Context clues: _____

   Meaning in context: _____ **Second meaning:** _____

3. "Let the rain beat upon your head with <u>silver</u> liquid drops."

   Context clues: _____

   Meaning in context: _____ **Second meaning:** _____

4. "The rain plays a little <u>sleep-song</u> on our roof at night—"

   Context clues: _____

   Meaning in context: _____ **Second meaning:** _____

Poetry Collection 2: Sandra Cisneros, Nikki Giovanni, Langston Hughes, Emily Dickinson
Literary Analysis: Figurative Language

Figurative language is language that is not meant to be taken literally. Authors use figurative language to state ideas in fresh ways. They may use one or more of the following types of figurative language:

- **Similes** compare two different things using the word *like* or *as:* "who throws coins like rain"
- **Metaphors** compare two different things by stating that one thing is another: "who is dough and feathers"
- **Personification** compares an object or animal to a human by giving it human characteristics: "Let the rain kiss you."

A. DIRECTIONS: *Underline each example of figurative language. Above the underlined phrase, write S if it is a simile, M if it is a metaphor, and P if it is personification. The first use of figurative language has been identified as an example.*

　　　　　P
The <u>pitiless sun</u> beat down on us like hammers as we walked home. The books in our

backpacks were as heavy as rocks. When we saw the fountain that welcomes visitors to the

park, we raced toward it. Our feet pounded on the stones leading to the center of the foun-

tain. We tore off our shoes and socks and splashed gratefully in the cool water. The fountain

was an oasis in the desert on that hot day.

B. DIRECTIONS: *Complete the following chart. First, identify the type of figurative language in each item. Then, tell what the figurative language does. Finally, tell what it shows. Look back at the poem if you need more context.*

Figurative Language	Type	What It Does	What It Shows
1. who tells me in English you are my sky ("Abuelito Who")	metaphor	It compares the speaker to the sky.	It shows how much Abuelito loves the speaker.
2. an ocean would never laugh ("The World Is Not a Pleasant Place to Be")			
3. Fame is a bee. It has a song— ("Fame is a Bee")			

Name _____ Date _____

Vocabulary Builder

Word List

    lullaby   pleasant   receive   sour

A. DIRECTIONS: *Think about the meaning of the underlined word in each item below. Then, answer the question, and explain your answer.*

1. If loading dock workers were ready to <u>receive</u> a shipment, what would they be doing?

   _____

   _____

2. If the milk is <u>sour</u>, what would you do with it?

   _____

   _____

3. If you had a <u>pleasant</u> time somewhere, would you go back again?

   _____

   _____

4. When a mother sings a <u>lullaby</u>, what might the baby do?

   _____

   _____

B. WORD STUDY: *The suffix* -ant *means "state or condition of being." Answer each of the following questions using one of these words containing* -ant: vigilant, important, ignorant.

1. Why does a doctor need to be *vigilant*?

   _____

2. Where would silence be *important*?

   _____

3. Why would an *ignorant* person be prone to making mistakes?

   _____

Name _____ Date _____

Poetry Collection 2: Sandra Cisneros, Nikki Giovanni, Langston Hughes, Emily Dickinson
Conventions: Comparisons With Adjectives and Adverbs

Most adjectives have different forms—the **positive** (strong), the **comparative** (stronger), and the **superlative** (strongest). *Comparative adjectives* are used to compare two people, places, or things. *Superlative adjectives* are used to compare three or more people, places, or things.

If a positive adjective contains one or two syllables, you can usually change it into a comparative or superlative adjective by adding the ending *-er* or *-est.* If the positive adjective contains three or more syllables, use the words *more* or *most.* For adverbs, use the words *more* or *most.*

Positive	Comparative	Superlative
tall (adj) slowly (adv)	This player is *taller* than that one. This dog runs *more slowly* than my dog.	These players are the *tallest* of all. Of the three animals, the sloth moves *most slowly* of all.
funny (adj) interesting (adjective with three or more syllables)	Your jokes are *funnier* than mine. (add -er to adjectives) Her story was *more interesting* than her sister's. (use *more*)	Her jokes are the *funniest* I've heard. (add -est to adjectives) The *most interesting* story is the last one in the book. (use *most*)

A few adjectives cannot take comparative or superlative forms. The adjective *unique* means "one of a kind" or "without equal." Something that is unique cannot be compared to anything else. These adjectives and adverbs are called *absolute modifiers.* Others include the words *original, complete,* and *perfect.*

A. PRACTICE: *In each of the following sentences, underline the comparative or superlative form of the adjective or adverb. Write* **C** *on the line if the sentence contains a comparative, and* **S** *if it contains a superlative. Write* **A** *if the sentence contains an absolute modifier.*

____ 1. Our fans display the team's colors more proudly than any other team's fans do.

____ 2. Of all those players, he performed most brilliantly.

____ 3. The pitcher and catcher were identical twins.

____ 4. Our pitcher is the fastest one in the league.

____ 5. The score was closer than they liked.

____ 6. The new stadium is more comfortable than the old one.

B. Writing Application: *Write a paragraph of five or more sentences about a sport you enjoy playing or watching. Use the comparative or superlative form of an adjective and of an adverb, each at least twice in the paragraph. Underline each comparative or superlative form that you use.*

_____

_____

Name _____ Date _____

Poetry Collection 2: Emily Dickinson, Langston Hughes, Sandra Cisneros, Nikki Giovanni
Support for Writing to Sources: Poem

Use this cluster diagram to gather ideas for a **poem** you will write using figurative language. First, write your subject in the oval at the center of the diagram. Then, in each circle around the oval, jot down one quality of your subject. Add more circles if you need them.

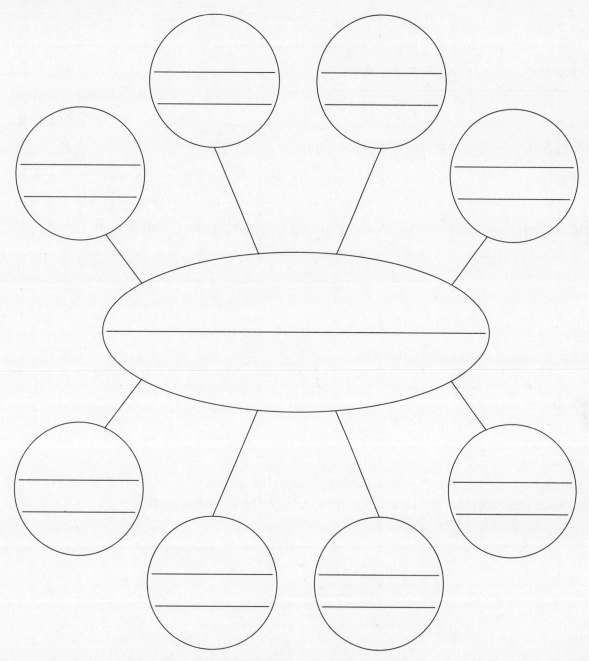

Now, use your notes to draft your poem. Be sure your poem has at least one simile, metaphor, or personification.

Poetry Collection 2: Sandra Cisneros, Nikki Giovanni, Langston Hughes, Emily Dickinson

Support for Speaking and Listening: Dramatic Poetry Reading

Answer these questions in preparation for your **poetry reading.**

Name of poem: _____

Where in the poem will I pause? _____

_____

_____

What words or lines will I read softly? _____

_____

_____

What words or lines will I read more loudly? _____

_____

_____

At what points in the poem will I show strong emotion? How should I read those parts?

_____

_____

_____

_____

Which words should I stress for effect? _____

_____

_____

_____

Now, practice reading your poem aloud using the notes you have made. Be sure to use appropriate gestures to emphasize important points in the poem.

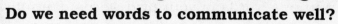

Poetry Collection 3
Bashō, Lillian Morrison, Anonymous, Dorthi Charles
Writing About the Big Question
Do we need words to communicate well?

Big Question Vocabulary

communicate	connection	correspond	dialogue	expression
gesture	language	message	nonverbal	quote
reveal	share	symbolize	verbal	visual

A. *Write one or more words from the list above to complete each sentence.*

1. A shrug is a _____ that can _____ confusion.

2. The mayor's refusal to compromise sent a strong _____ to the Town Council.

3. A witness told the journalist, "You may _____ me in your article, but please don't use my name."

B. *Follow the directions in responding to each of the items below.*

1. What might a person's reading preferences **reveal** about him or her?

_____

_____

2. Write two sentences that describe the genre of literature you like best. Use at least two Big Question vocabulary words.

_____

_____

C. *Complete the sentence below. Then, write a short paragraph in which you connect this idea to the Big Question by explaining how poetry uses words to communicate well.*

The language of poetry is unique because _____

_____

_____

_____

_____

_____

_____

_____

Poetry Collection 3: Bashō, Anonymous, Lillian Morrison, Dorthi Charles

Reading: Paraphrasing

Paraphrasing is restating an author's words in your own words. Paraphrasing difficult or confusing passages in a poem helps you clarify the meaning. Use these steps to help you:

- First, stop and reread any difficult lines or passages.
- Next, identify unfamiliar words. Find their meaning and replace them with words that mean the same or nearly the same thing.
- Then, restate the lines in your own words, using everyday speech.
- Finally, reread the lines to see if your paraphrase makes sense in the poem.

A chart such as the one below can be useful in helping you paraphrase.

DIRECTIONS: *In the left column of the chart are passages from the poems in this collection. Underline unfamiliar words. Find the meanings of these words and write the meaning in the second column. In the third column, paraphrase the passage. The first one has been done for you as an example.*

Passage	New Words	Paraphrase
Example: <u>Skimming</u> an <u>asphalt</u> sea	skimming: moving swiftly; asphalt: pavement	gliding swiftly over the sidewalk
1. I swerve, I curve, I sway;		
2. An old silent pond . . .		
3. There was a young fellow named Hall, Who fell in the spring in the fall;		
4. 'Twould have been a sad thing If he'd died in the spring, But he didn't—he died in the fall.		

Poetry Collection 3: Bashō, Anonymous, Lillian Morrison, Dorthi Charles

Literary Analysis: Forms of Poetry

Poets use different **forms of poetry** suited to the ideas, images, and feelings they want to express. The following are three poetic forms:

- A **haiku** is a Japanese verse form with three lines. Line 1 has five syllables, line 2 has seven syllables, and line 3 has five syllables. Haiku often focuses on nature. It tries to capture a moment by giving you a few quick images or word pictures that help you see and hear something in a new way.
- A **limerick** is a short, funny poem of five lines. The first, second, and fifth lines rhyme and have three beats, or stressed syllables. The third and fourth lines rhyme and have two strong beats.
- A **concrete poem** has words arranged in a shape that reflects the subject of the poem.

DIRECTIONS: *Answer the questions about each form of poetry below.*

1. "Haiku" by Bashō

	What do you see?	**What do you hear?**
An old silent pond . . .		
A frog jumps into the pond,		
splash! Silence again.		

2. "Limerick" by Anonymous

Underline each *stressed* syllable in each line. Then, identify the rhyme scheme or pattern by writing the letters *a* or *b* at the end of each line. Give each rhyme a different letter. For example, write the letter *a* at the end of the first line and *a* at the end of each line that rhymes with line one.

There was a young fellow named Hall, _____

Who fell in the spring in the fall; _____

'Twould have been a sad thing _____

If he'd died in the spring, _____

But he didn't—he died in the fall. _____

3. "The Sidewalk Racer" by Lillian Morrison and "Concrete Cat" by Dorthi Charles

Concrete means "something real, something that can be touched," such as an apple, a tree, or a cellphone. List three subjects that you think might be good choices for a concrete poem.

_____

_____

_____

Poetry Collection 3: Bashō, Lillian Morrison, Anonymous, Dorthi Charles

Vocabulary Builder

Word List

   asphalt   fellow   skimming

A. DIRECTIONS: *Revise each sentence to use the underlined vocabulary word logically. Be sure to keep the vocabulary word in your revision.*

1. His dishonesty earned him his reputation as a good <u>fellow</u>.

   _____

   _____

2. The skaters had a difficult time <u>skimming</u> over the smooth ice.

   _____

   _____

3. People use <u>asphalt</u> to surface buildings.

   _____

   _____

B. WORD STUDY: *The* Greek prefix *auto-* means "self." *Answer each of the following questions using one of these words containing* auto-: autopilot, autographed, automatic.

1. When is an airplane flying on *autopilot*?

   _____

2. In what way might a star's *autographed* picture become valuable?

   _____

3. How does an *automatic* spell checker help you as you type on a computer?

   _____

Poetry Collection 3: Bashō, Anonymous, Lillian Morrison, Dorthi Charles

Conventions: Conjunctions and Interjections

Conjunctions: A **conjunction** is a word that connects sentence parts and shows the relationship between them.

- **Shows an additional idea or event:** We read a great story in class, *and* I wrote a poem about it.
- **Shows a contrasting idea or event:** I like my poem, *but* I can't think of a good title for it.
- **Shows a choice between ideas or events:** I will try again tomorrow, *or* I will ask my classmates for ideas.

A. PRACTICE: *Circle the conjunction in each sentence. Underline the sentence parts that each conjunction connects.*

1. Limericks are very clever, and they make me laugh.
2. Rain was falling, yet the sun was shining brightly.
3. The character in that story loves solitude, so he spends time in the forest.
4. Are you going to the movies, or will you stay home tonight?

Interjections: An **interjection** is a word or group of words that expresses sudden excitement or strong feeling. A strong interjection is followed by an exclamation point. A comma follows a mild interjection. When the interjection is followed by a comma, it is connected to the sentence that follows it.

Strong interjection—separated from following sentence: *Wait!* Please take me with you.

Mild interjection—connected to following sentence: *Well,* maybe it is time to go.

B. PRACTICE: *Circle the interjection in each of the following sentences. Then, write whether it is a strong interjection or mild interjection.*

1. Cool! Did you see that frog jump? _____
2. Oh, no! The skater has fallen! _____
3. Hey, a few bumps and bruises can be expected. _____

C. Writing Application: *Write a brief account of an experience you had watching a sporting event. Use at least two conjunctions and two interjections in your account. Underline those parts of speech.*

_____

_____

_____

_____

_____

Poetry Collection 3: Bashō, Anonymous, Lillian Morrison, Dorthi Charles

Support for Writing to Sources: Poem

You have read examples of a haiku, a limerick, and a concrete poem. Now, try writing a poem of your own, using one of these forms.

What form of poetry will you use? _____

What do you need to remember about this form? Take notes here.

_____

_____

_____

_____

Use the lines below to jot down ideas for your poem. If you're writing a haiku, you will want to think about nature images. If you're writing a limerick, think up a silly character or start with place names that sound funny and will be easy to rhyme—for example, "Chicago." If you're writing a concrete poem, think of a real subject that suggests a shape—for example, a pizza or an ocean wave.

_____

_____

_____

_____

_____

_____

_____

_____

_____

_____

_____

_____

_____

_____

_____

Poetry Collection 3: Bashō, Anonymous, Lillian Morrison, Dorthi Charles

Support for Research and Technology: Presentation of Poem

Decide which of the four poems you will format, and then use the space below to design your presentation.

Name _____   Date _____

William Shakespeare, Gwendolyn Brooks, Shel Silverstein, and Octavio Paz

Writing About the Big Question

Do we need words to communicate well?

Big Question Vocabulary

communicate	connection	correspond	dialogue	expression
gesture	language	message	nonverbal	quote
reveal	share	symbolize	verbal	visual

A. *Write a word from the list above to complete each sentence.*

1. What is the _____ between your answer and my question?

2. I like to text message to _____ with my friends.

3. Even though your words are pleasant, your _____ cues are not.

4. If we _____ our ideas, we can solve this problem.

B. *Follow the directions in responding to each of the items below.*

1. Must a poem be about something you have experienced for you to make a **connection** to it? Why or why not?

_____

_____

2. In two sentences, describe the qualities you enjoy in a poem. Use at least two Big Question vocabulary words.

_____

_____

C. *Complete the sentence below. Then, write a short paragraph in which you connect this idea to the Big Question.*

Reading about someone else's experiences helps the reader to feel a connection to

_____

_____

_____

_____

_____

Name _____ Date _____

Reading: Paraphrasing

Paraphrasing is restating something in your own words. To paraphrase a poem, you must first understand it and then use simpler language to restate its meaning. **Reading aloud according to punctuation** will help you find clues to a poem's meaning.

- When you read a poem aloud, do not automatically stop at the end of each line.
- Pause only at punctuation marks, as if you were reading a prose passage.

Even when you read poetry silently to yourself, it will make more sense if you follow these rules:

- **No punctuation** at the ends of lines: don't stop
- **After a comma (,):** slight pause
- **After a colon (:), semicolon (;), or dash (—):** longer pause
- **After endmarks—a period (.), question mark (?), or exclamation point (!):** full stop

A. DIRECTIONS: *Below are the first five lines from the poem "Cynthia in the Snow." For each line, write the letters* SP *for slight pause,* LP *for longer pause,* FS *for full stop, or* DS *for don't stop. The first line has been done for you as an example.*

Line 1: It SUSHES.   FS
Line 2: It hushes   _____
Line 3: The loudness in the road.   _____
Line 4: It flitter-twitters,   _____
Line 5: And laughs away from me.   _____

B. DIRECTIONS: *Briefly explain why a good reader will not pause between lines 2 and 3.*

_____

_____

_____

_____

_____

_____

_____

_____

_____

_____

_____

_____

Name _____ Date _____

Literary Analysis: Sound Devices

Sound devices are a writer's tools for bringing out the music in words and for expressing feelings. Sound devices commonly used in poetry include the following:

- **Repetition:** the use, more than once, of any element of language—a sound, word, phrase, clause, or sentence—as in *This land is your land/ This land is my land*
- **Alliteration:** the repetition of initial consonant sounds, such as the *b* sound in *beautiful big brown eyes* or the *cl* sound in *clattered* and *clashed*
- **Onomatopoeia:** the use of a word that sounds like what it means, such as *patter* and *roar*

A. DIRECTIONS: *Underline the repetition, alliteration, and onomatopoeia in the following lines from the poetry collection. On the line after each item, write R for repetition, A for alliteration, and O for onomatopoeia. Some items will have more than one letter. The first one has been done for you.*

1. You <u>spotted snakes</u> with double tongue   <u>   A   </u>
2. Lulla, lulla, lullaby, lulla, lulla lullaby   _____
3. The water runs off and is wind.   _____
4. No more smell of kitty litter, / No more mousies in my bed.   _____
5. It SUSHES   _____
6. And whitely whirs away   _____

B. DIRECTIONS: *Find one example of repetition, one example of alliteration, and one example of onomatopoeia in this passage. Then, write the examples on the lines below.*

There would be no stargazing, no night hike, and no campfire until the weather cleared. We scrambled into our sleeping bags, determined to get some rest. The drip, drip, drip of the rain on the roof of the tent finally put us to sleep. We woke up suddenly when we heard Roy shouting outside. We unzipped the tent and saw a big, brown bear standing on its hind legs at the edge of the woods. We grabbed pans and banged on them as the bear crashed through the bushes to escape the noise.

1. Example of repetition: _____

2. Example of alliteration: _____

3. Example of onomatopoeia: _____

Name _____ Date _____

Poetry Collection 4: William Shakespeare, Gwendolyn Brooks, Shel Silverstein, Octavio Paz

Vocabulary Builder

Word List

dispersed   hollowed   offense   sculpted   thorny   whirs

A. Directions: *Following the instructions, use each Word List word correctly.*

1. Use *dispersed* in a sentence about the effects of a sudden rainstorm at a parade.

   _____

   _____

2. Use *offense* in a sentence about a misunderstanding.

   _____

   _____

3. Use *hollowed* in a sentence about carving a pumpkin.

   _____

   _____

4. Use *sculpted* in a sentence about something made of wood.

   _____

   _____

5. Use *whirs* in a sentence about a breeze.

   _____

   _____

6. Use *thorny* in a sentence about a hike through a thick forest.

   _____

   _____

B. Word Study: *The suffix -y forms adjectives that mean "having, full of, or characterized by." Answer each of the following questions using one of these words containing -y: hearty, stealthy, thorny.*

1. What is one plant that could be considered *thorny?*

   _____

2. What would be someone's feelings toward you if that person gives you a *hearty* welcome?

   _____

3. What kind of animal has a *stealthy* approach when hunting prey?

   _____

Poetry Collection 4: William Shakespeare, Gwendolyn Brooks, Shel Silverstein, Octavio Paz
Conventions: Sentence Parts and Types

Sentence Parts

A sentence consists of a **subject** and a **predicate** and expresses a complete thought. A **simple subject** is the person, place, or thing about which the sentence is written. A **complete subject** includes the simple subject and any related words. A **simple predicate** is the verb that expresses the main action. A **complete predicate** includes the verb and any related words. In this example, the simple subject and verb are in bold type. The complete subject is underlined once; the complete predicate, twice.

<u>Octavio Paz, a Mexican poet,</u> <u>**won** the 1990 Nobel Prize for Literature.</u>

Sentence Types

Sentences can be classified according to their function or purpose. Notice that every sentence begins with a capital letter and ends with a punctuation mark. The kind of punctuation mark that is used depends on the function of the sentence.

Type	Function and End Punctuation	Example
Declarative	makes a statement; ends with a period	These poems are interesting.
Interrogative	asks a question; ends with a question mark	Which poem do you like best?
Imperative	gives an order or a direction; ends with a period or an exclamation point	Let us read this poem. Please bring me that book. Catch it before it falls!
Exclamatory	expresses strong emotion; ends with an exclamation point	What an imaginaton this poet has!

A. PRACTICE: *Classify these sentences by writing* declarative, interrogative, imperative, *or* exclamatory *on the line provided. Then, circle the simple subject and underline the simple predicate.*

1. What a wonderful poem that is! _____
2. Elena, please read the first poem in this collection. _____
3. These poems are about nature, and those are about people. _____
4. Does anyone have anything to add? _____

B. Writing Application: *Write one of each type of sentence. For the declarative sentence, underline the complete subject once and the complete predicate twice.*

_____

_____

_____

_____

Name _____ Date _____

Support for Writing to Sources: Prose Description

Choose one of the poems, and use the chart to list details for a prose description of the picture the poet painted. The list will help you focus on details that appeal to the senses.

Details I Might See:
Details I Might Smell:
Details I Might Hear:
Details I Might Touch or Be Able to Feel:
Details I Might Taste:

Now, use the details you have collected to write your prose description.

Name _____ Date _____

Poetry Collection 4: Shel Silverstein, Octavio Paz, William Shakespeare, Gwendolyn Brooks
Support for Research and Technology: Résumé

Use the chart to record the facts for the résumé of the poet you have chosen.

Name of Poet: _____

Personal Information (birthplace, childhood, family, travel, hobbies, interests):
Education:
Career Accomplishments:
Books or Poems Published/Awards:

Now, use a word-processing program to correctly format the résumé.

Poetry by Robert Frost and E. E. Cummings
Writing About the Big Question

Do we need words to communicate well?

Big Question Vocabulary

communicate	connection	correspond	dialogue	expression
gesture	language	message	nonverbal	quote
reveal	share	symbolize	verbal	visual

A. *Write a word from the list above to complete each sentence.*

1. Do items in poems always _____ feelings and ideas?

2. Poetic images are _____ if they create pictures in readers' minds.

3. Sometimes it's easier to _____ feelings by writing about them than by talking about them.

4. A person's _____ might appear sad even if he or she is content.

B. *Follow the directions in responding to each of the items below.*

1. Tell whether you more often read poems, which **communicate through words**, or look at paintings, which **communicate visually**. Explain your choice.

   _____

   _____

2. Write two sentences that describe the difference between a poem and a painting that you find most striking. Use at least two Big Question vocabulary words.

   _____

   _____

C. *Complete the sentence below. Then, write a short paragraph in which you connect this idea to the Big Question.*

A visual image can be conveyed through words or pictures, but I prefer _____

   _____

   _____

   _____

   _____

Name _____   Date _____

Poetry by Robert Frost and E.E. Cummings
Literary Analysis: Imagery

An **image** is a word or phrase that appeals to one of the five senses of sight, hearing, smell, taste, or touch. An image can also create a feeling of movement.

Writers use this sensory language—**imagery**—to create word pictures. The imagery in a word picture can appeal to more than one sense. For example, the images in the following lines appeal to the senses of both touch and taste:

Cold hands, warm mug;

sip of cocoa, mother's hug . . .

Imagery also helps a writer express mood. **Mood** is the feeling that a poem creates in a reader. A poem's mood might be fanciful, thoughtful, or lonely. In the lines above, the poet uses images that create a mood of cozy affection.

A. DIRECTIONS: *Listed below are images from Robert Frost's poem "Dust of Snow" and E.E. Cummings's poem "who knows if the moon's." For each image, list the senses that are involved. Choose from sight, hearing, smell, taste, and touch. Also, explain whether the image creates a feeling of movement. Remember that each image can appeal to more than one sense.*

"Dust of Snow"	
Image	**Senses**
1. crow shaking branches of tree	
2. dust of snow falling on speaker	

"who knows if the moon's"	
Image	**Senses**
3. the moon as a balloon	
4. a balloon filled with pretty people	
5. going up above houses and steeples and clouds	
6. flowers picking themselves	

B. DIRECTIONS: *Tell what mood, or feeling, each poem's images help create.*

1. The mood of "Dust of Snow" is _____

2. The mood of "who knows if the moon's" is _____

Name _____ Date _____

"who knows if the moon's" by E. E. Cummings
"Dust of Snow" by Robert Frost

Vocabulary Builder

Word List

rued   steeples

A. DIRECTIONS: *For each of the following, write* T *if the statement is true or if it makes sense, or write* F *if the statement is false or does not make sense.*

_____ 1. From the top of the *steeple*, you can see for miles.

_____ 2. My parents *rued* the day I got straight A's on my report card.

_____ 3. *Steeples* are usually made of wooden toothpicks.

_____ 4. Many churches have *steeples*.

_____ 5. The day I *rued* most was the day I left a door open and our cat ran away.

B. DIRECTIONS: *Fill in the following word map for the word* rue.

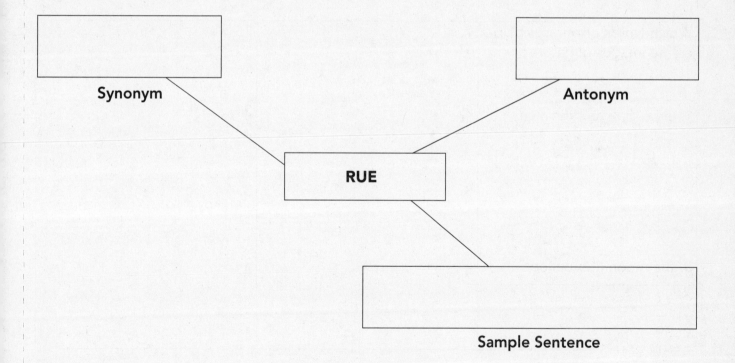

Synonym

Antonym

RUE

Sample Sentence

All-in-One Workbook
157

Poetry by Robert Frost and E.E. Cummings
Support for Writing to Compare Imagery

Before you draft your essay comparing the role of nature in each poem, complete the graphic organizer below.

Nature	"Dust of Snow"	"who knows if the moon's"
Is nature seen as positive or negative?		
Does nature play a central role or a background role?		
Which words or phrases help create images of nature?	1. 2. 3. 4.	1. 2. 3. 4.

Now, use your notes to write an essay comparing the role nature plays in each poem. Be sure to include examples from the poems to support your ideas.

Writing Process
Argumentative Essay

Prewriting: Gathering Details

Use the following chart to list facts, examples, statistics, quotations, and personal observations that support your claim. List all sources that you use in order to give credit for any ideas or words that are not your own.

Claim: _____

Evidence that supports your claim:	Sources used and consulted during research:

Drafting: Organizing Clearly

Use the following chart to organize ideas clearly and concisely for your essay.

Introduction (including thesis statement)	
Body Paragraph 1 (including facts, details, and other support for the first reason for your claim)	
Body Paragraph 2 (including facts, details, and other support for the second reason for your claim)	
Body Paragraph 3 (including facts, details, and other support for the third reason for your claim)	
Conclusion (including a restatement of your thesis)	

Writer's Toolbox
Conventions: Coordinating Conjunctions

Combining Sentences Using Coordinating Conjunctions

You can join a pair of short, related sentences with coordinating conjunctions. First, determine the relationship between the ideas in your sentences. Then, choose the coordinating conjunction that fits your meaning and purpose.

Conjunction	Purpose	Use
and	to join similar or related ideas	The park is large, **and** the lake nearby is beautiful.
but	to highlight differences	The shops are open, **but** the banks are closed.
or	to show choices	You can take a bus to the airport, **or** you can call a taxi.
so	to show cause and effect	At last, the pond was frozen, **so** the skaters took to the ice.

A. PRACTICE: *On the line, write the conjunction that makes the best sense in the sentence.*

1. My dad came to watch me play, _____ my mom had to work late.

2. I scored two goals, _____ my friend Clarissa scored two also.

3. We can win this game, _____ we can lose.

4. We were ahead until the last two minutes, _____ then we made too many fouls.

B. WRITING APPLICATION: *On the lines provided, combine the sentences using a coordinating conjunction.*

1. I like baseball. Wilbert likes basketball.

   _____

2. Basketball is a fast-paced game. Players who can pass do well.

   _____

3. Wilbert's skills make him a quick player. He is usually a starter.

   _____

4. My sister may take gymnastics. She may sign up for tennis instead.

   _____

Name _____ Date _____

"Simile: Willow and Ginkgo" by Eve Merriam
Vocabulary Builder

Selection Vocabulary

crude   stubby   thrives

A. DIRECTIONS: *Look at the italicized word in each sentence. Then, explain whether each sentence makes sense. If the sentence does not make sense, write a new sentence using the word correctly.*

1. My dad and mom built a strong, well-designed tree house that everyone said was *crude*.

   _____

2. The rosebush *thrives* in the dark with little water.

   _____

3. The *stubby* bushes will probably not get much bigger, because they are shaded by the taller bushes and trees.

   _____

Academic Vocabulary

communicate   establish   reveal

B. DIRECTIONS: *Write two different sentences for each of the following words. Try to use the word to explain something entirely different in your second sentence.*

   Example: The chairperson maintained tight <u>control</u> of the discussion.
   Scientists often use <u>control</u> groups in their studies.

COMMUNICATE

1. _____
2. _____

ESTABLISH

3. _____
4. _____

REVEAL

5. _____
6. _____

Name _____ Date _____

"**Simile: Willow and Ginkgo**" by Eve Merriam
Take Notes for Discussion

Before the Group Discussion: Read the passage from the selection in your textbook.

The willow's music is like a soprano, . . . everyone joining in.

During the Discussion: As the group discusses each question, take notes on how other students' ideas either differ from or build upon your own.

Discussion Questions	Other Responses	Comparison to My Responses
1. Why does the speaker describe the ginkgo's music as a "chorus"?		
2. Which is more positive, the description of the willow's music or of the ginkgo's tune? Why?		

"Simile: Willow and Ginkgo" by Eve Merriam
Take Notes for Writing to Sources

Planning Your Informative Text: Before you begin drafting your **expository essay**, use the chart below to organize your ideas.

Introduction to poem and statement of thesis:

_____

_____

_____

_____

_____

_____

Details about the qualities of a particular environment and the way it creates a need for determination:

_____

_____

_____

_____

_____

_____

Notes about the relationship between the environment and determination for your conclusion:

_____

_____

_____

_____

_____

_____

Name _____ Date _____

"Simile: Willow and Ginkgo" by Eve Merriam
Take Notes for Research

As you research **what social scientists have learned about factors that help children use determination to make positive choices and thrive in their environments,** use the forms below to take notes from your sources. As necessary, continue your notes on the back of this page, on note cards, or in a word-processing document.

Source Information   Check one: ☐ Primary Source   ☐ Secondary Source

Title: _____   Author: _____

Publication Information: _____

Page(s): _____

Main Idea: _____

_____

Quotation or Paraphrase: _____

_____

Source Information   Check one: ☐ Primary Source   ☐ Secondary Source

Title: _____   Author: _____

Publication Information: _____

Page(s): _____

Main Idea: _____

_____

Quotation or Paraphrase: _____

_____

Source Information   Check one: ☐ Primary Source   ☐ Secondary Source

Title: _____   Author: _____

Publication Information: _____

Page(s): _____

Main Idea: _____

_____

Quotation or Paraphrase: _____

_____

Name _____ Date _____

"Angela Duckworth and the Research on 'Grit'" by Emily Hanford
Vocabulary Builder

Selection Vocabulary

insurmountable   persevere   rigorous

A. DIRECTIONS: *Write at least one synonym, one antonym, and an example sentence for each word. Synonyms and antonyms can be words or phrases.*

Word	Synonym	Antonym	Example Sentence
insurmountable			
persevere			
rigorous			

Academic Vocabulary

essential   research   study

B. DIRECTIONS: *Write two different sentences for each of the vocabulary words. Try to use the word to explain something entirely different in your second sentence.*

Example: The chairperson maintained tight <u>control</u> of the discussion.
Scientists often use <u>control</u> groups in their studies.

ESSENTIAL

1. _____

2. _____

RESEARCH

3. _____

4. _____

STUDY

5. _____

6. _____

Name _____ Date _____

Take Notes for Discussion

Before the Discussion: Read the passage from the selection in your text that begins and ends as shown below.

Donald Kamentz, director of college initiatives . . . when it comes to college.

During the Discussion: As you discuss each question with your partner, take notes on how your partner's ideas either differ from or build upon your own.

Discussion Questions	Other Ideas Expressed	Comparison to My Own Ideas
1. What makes some gritty people "not gritty enough when it comes to college"?		
2. Why might people be gritty about some things and not others?		

Name _____ Date _____

"Angela Duckworth and the Research on 'Grit'" by Emily Hanford

Take Notes for Research

As you research **what factors can cause students to drop out of college,** use the chart below to take notes from your sources. As necessary, continue your notes on the back of this page, on note cards, or in a word-processing document.

Causes of Students Dropping Out of College	
Main Idea _____ _____	Main Idea _____ _____
Quotation or Paraphrase _____ _____ _____ _____	Quotation or Paraphrase _____ _____ _____ _____
Source Information _____ _____ _____ _____	Source Information _____ _____ _____ _____
Main Idea _____ _____	Main Idea _____ _____
Quotation or Paraphrase _____ _____ _____ _____	Quotation or Paraphrase _____ _____ _____ _____
Source Information _____ _____ _____	Source Information _____ _____ _____

"Angela Duckworth and the Research on 'Grit'" by Emily Hanford
Take Notes for Writing to Sources

Planning Your Narrative: Before you begin drafting your **autobiographical narrative**, use the chart below to organize your ideas.

---

1. Notes for your introduction, including an explanation of the meaning of grit and a situation in which you needed it:

_____

_____

_____

_____

---

2. Notes about how you used grit in the situation:

_____

_____

_____

_____

_____

_____

_____

_____

---

3. Notes about literary elements that you will use to create an engaging narrative:

_____

_____

_____

_____

---

4. Notes for your conclusion in which you connect your "gritty" experience with the experiences of people in Hanford's article.

_____

_____

_____

_____

Name _____ Date _____

Selection Vocabulary

expedition   plateau   polar

A. DIRECTIONS: *Think about the meaning of the italicized word in each question below. Then, write the answer.*

1. If you were planning an *expedition*, would you need to pack a suitcase? Why or why not?

   _____

2. What is one item you would need to take on a trip to a *polar* region? Explain your answer.

   _____

3. If you were hiking on a *plateau*, would you expect to get out of breath and tired? Explain your answer.

   _____

Academic Vocabulary

assess   evidence   perspective

B. DIRECTIONS: *On the line, write whether each sentence is true or false, and then explain your answer.*

_____ 1. Scientists usually *assess* the results of their research.

   _____

_____ 2. Supporting your argument with *evidence* is not a good idea.

   _____

_____ 3. *Perspective* is not important when telling a story.

   _____

Name _____ Date _____

"Race to the End of the Earth" by William G. Scheller
Take Notes for Discussion

Before the Group Discussion: Read the passage from the selection in your text that begins and ends as show below.

> The drifts were so deep and the snow was falling so heavily . . . their goal: the South Pole.

During the Discussion: As you discuss each question, take notes on how other students' ideas either differ from or build upon your own.

Discussion Questions	Other Ideas Expressed	Comparison to My Own Ideas
1. How does the author emphasize the danger of South Pole expeditions?		
2. How does this passage relate to the idea of determination?		

Name _____ Date _____

Take Notes for Research

As you research **to learn more about Scott's background and to find out whether or not Scott and his team ever reached the South Pole,** use the chart below to take notes from your sources. As necessary, continue your notes on the back of this page, on note cards, or in a word-processing document.

Robert Scott and the South Pole	
Main Idea _____ Quotation or Paraphrase _____ _____ _____ _____ Source Information _____ _____ _____ _____	Main Idea _____ Quotation or Paraphrase _____ _____ _____ _____ Source Information _____ _____ _____ _____
Main Idea _____ Quotation or Paraphrase _____ _____ _____ _____ Source Information _____ _____ _____ _____	Main Idea _____ Quotation or Paraphrase _____ _____ _____ _____ Source Information _____ _____ _____ _____

"Race to the End of the Earth" by William G. Scheller
Take Notes for Writing to Sources

Planning Your Diary Entry: Before you begin drafting your **diary entry,** use the chart below to organize your ideas.

---

1. Notes about vivid language that will describe your experiences:

_____

_____

_____

_____

_____

_____

---

2. Notes for expanding information from the text:

_____

_____

_____

_____

_____

_____

_____

_____

_____

_____

---

3. Transitions that will build suspense and connect your ideas:

_____

_____

_____

_____

_____

Name _____ Date _____

"The Sound of Summer Running" from *Dandelion Wine* by Ray Bradbury
Vocabulary Builder

Selection Vocabulary

revelation   seized   suspended

A. DIRECTIONS: *Each sentence below contains an italicized vocabulary word. Explain whether each sentence makes sense, given the meaning of the italicized word. If the sentence does not make sense, write a new sentence using the word correctly.*

1. Because of his *revelation*, he was not able to understand how to work the math problem.

   _____

2. The other team *seized* the ball and was able to score.

   _____

3. School was *suspended*, so we all hurried to get to our classes.

   _____

Academic Vocabulary

influence   symbolize

B. DIRECTIONS: *Write two different sentences for each of the vocabulary words. If you wish, you may use different forms of the word for your second sentence.*

   Example: Most voters <u>rejected</u> the proposed tax increase.
   The <u>rejection</u> of the tax proposal disappointed many people.

1. influence: _____

   _____

2. symbolize: _____

   _____

Name _____ Date _____

"The Sound of Summer Running" from *Dandelion Wine* by Ray Bradbury
Take Notes for Discussion

Before the Group Discussion: Read the following passage from the selection.

He held his coin bank up and heard the faint small tinkling, the airy weight of money there. . . .

Whatever you want, he thought, you got to make your own way. During the night now, let's find that path through the forest . . .

Downtown, the store lights went out, one by one. A wind blew in the window. It was like a river going downstream and his feet wanting to go with it.

During the Discussion: As you discuss each question, take notes on how other students' ideas either differ from or build upon your own.

Discussion Questions	Other Ideas Expressed	Comparison to My Own Ideas
1. Why does Douglas think that "you got to make your own way"?		
2. How does the wind influence Douglas's determination?		

"The Sound of Summer Running" from *Dandelion Wine* by Ray Bradbury
Take Notes for Research

As you research **to find out how young people can learn financial, or money-related, skills,** you can use the forms below. As necessary, continue your notes on the back of this page, on note cards, or in a word-processing document.

How to Learn Financial Skills	
Main Idea _____ _____ **Quotation or Paraphrase** _____ _____ _____ _____ _____ **Source Information** _____ _____ _____ _____	**Main Idea** _____ _____ **Quotation or Paraphrase** _____ _____ _____ _____ _____ **Source Information** _____ _____ _____ _____
Main Idea _____ _____ **Quotation or Paraphrase** _____ _____ _____ _____ _____ **Source Information** _____ _____ _____ _____	**Main Idea** _____ _____ **Quotation or Paraphrase** _____ _____ _____ _____ _____ **Source Information** _____ _____ _____ _____

"The Sound of Summer Running" from *Dandelion Wine* by Ray Bradbury
Take Notes for Writing to Sources

Planning Your Narrative: Before you begin drafting your **autobiographical narrative**, use the chart below to organize your ideas.

1. Notes for your introduction, including identification of something that has symbolic meaning for you:

_____

_____

_____

_____

_____

_____

2. Notes about how the item developed its meaning:

_____

_____

_____

_____

_____

_____

_____

_____

_____

3. Notes for your conclusion, in which you make connections between your symbolic object and Douglas's shoes:

_____

_____

_____

_____

_____

Name _____ Date _____

Selection Vocabulary

explicit   felicity   procure

A. DIRECTIONS: *Write the letter of the word or phrase that is the best synonym for the italicized word. Then, use the italicized word in a complete sentence.*

_____ 1. *explicit*

    A. extra   **C.** permit

    B. clear   **D.** expressive

_____

_____ 2. *felicity*

    A. ability to find proper expression   **C.** ability to agree on
       for one's thoughts   an idea

    B. ability to vote   **D.** ability to rule

_____

_____ 3. *procure*

    A. begin again   **C.** obtain

    B. stop   **D.** go ahead

_____

Academic Vocabulary

clarifies   contrasts   evaluate

B. DIRECTIONS: *Revise each sentence so that the italicized vocabulary word is used logically. Be sure not to change the vocabulary word.*

1. The teacher's explanation *clarifies* the math problem, so now I cannot solve it.

_____

2. Before we *evaluate* the team's chances, we should risk changing the lineup.

_____

3. His attitude toward the environment *contrasts* with mine, so we completely agree.

_____

Name _____ Date _____

from "Letter on Thomas Jefferson" by John Adams
Take Notes for Discussion

Before the Group Discussion: Read the passage from the selection in your text that begins and ends as show below.

> I said, "I will not. … You can write ten times better than I can."

During the Discussion: As you discuss each question, take notes on how other students' ideas either differ from or build upon your own.

Discussion Questions	Other Ideas Expressed	Comparison to My Own Ideas
1. Do you think Adams's version of the conversation matches what was really said? Why or why not?	_____ _____ _____ _____ _____ _____ _____ _____ _____ _____ _____	_____ _____ _____ _____ _____ _____ _____ _____ _____ _____ _____
2. How does Adams's version of the conversation characterize Adams himself?	_____ _____ _____ _____ _____ _____ _____ _____ _____ _____	_____ _____ _____ _____ _____ _____ _____ _____ _____ _____

Name _____ Date _____

from **"Letter on Thomas Jefferson"** by John Adams
Take Notes for Research

As you research **to learn about the process that the Continental Congress followed in order to write and approve the Declaration of Independence,** you can use the organizer below to take notes from your sources. As necessary, continue your notes on the back of this page, on note cards, or in a word-processing document.

Source Information   Check one: ☐ Primary Source   ☐ Secondary Source

Title: _____   Author: _____

Publication Information: _____

Page(s): _____

Main Idea: _____

_____

Quotation or Paraphrase: _____

_____

Source Information   Check one: ☐ Primary Source   ☐ Secondary Source

Title: _____   Author: _____

Publication Information: _____

Page(s): _____

Main Idea: _____

_____

Quotation or Paraphrase: _____

_____

Source Information   Check one: ☐ Primary Source   ☐ Secondary Source

Title: _____   Author: _____

Publication Information: _____

Page(s): _____

Main Idea: _____

_____

Quotation or Paraphrase: _____

_____

Name _____ Date _____

from **"Letter on Thomas Jefferson"** by John Adams
Take Notes for Writing to Sources

Planning Your Argument: Before you begin drafting your **comparison-and-contrast essay,** use the chart below to organize your ideas.

Details About Adams and Jefferson from Adams's Letter	
Adams	**Jefferson**
_____	_____
_____	_____
_____	_____
_____	_____
_____	_____
_____	_____
_____	_____
_____	_____

1. Notes about the organization of your essay to show similarities and differences:

_____

_____

_____

_____

_____

2. Transitional words and phrases that will show comparisons and contrasts:

_____

_____

_____

_____

_____

_____

Name _____   Date _____

"**Water**" by Helen Keller
Vocabulary Builder

Selection Vocabulary

barriers   imitate   persisted

A. DIRECTIONS: *Each sentence below includes an italicized word from the vocabulary list. Explain whether each sentence makes sense, given the meaning of the italicized word. If it does not make sense, write a new sentence using the word correctly.*

1. When they removed the *barriers* from the road, we were prevented from driving on.

   _____

2. My little sister likes to *imitate* me, so she wears my clothes.

   _____

3. Lorenzo *persisted* in learning to speak French, so it's no wonder that he cannot carry on a conversation in the language.

   _____

Academic Vocabulary

purpose   sources   support

B. DIRECTIONS: *Write two different sentences for each of the following words. Try to use the word in a different way in each sentence.*

> **Example:** From the kitchen came the <u>fragrance</u> of freshly baked apple pie.
> The forest was dense with <u>fragrant</u> pine trees.

1. purpose: _____

   _____

2. sources: _____

   _____

3. support: _____

   _____

Name _____   Date _____

"**Water**" by Helen Keller
Take Notes for Discussion

Before the Small Group Discussion: Read the passage from the selection in your textbook that begins and ends as shown below.

> Running downstairs to my mother, I held up my hand and made the letters for doll. . . . I understood that everything has a name.

During the Discussion: As the group discusses each question, take notes on how other students' ideas either differ from or build upon your own.

Discussion Questions	Other Ideas Expressed	Comparison to My Own Ideas
1. In this passage, how does Keller show determination?		
2. How will her determination aid her in years to come?		

Name _____   Date _____

"**Water**" by Helen Keller
Take Notes for Research

As you research **how people with visual impairments learn to read, or how people with hearing impairments learn to communicate without speaking**, you can use the organizer below to take notes from your sources. As necessary, continue your notes on the back of this page, on note cards, or in a word-processing document.

Source Information   Check one: ☐ Primary Source   ☐ Secondary Source

Title: _____   Author: _____

Publication Information: _____

Page(s): _____

Main Idea: _____

_____

Quotation or Paraphrase: _____

_____

Source Information   Check one: ☐ Primary Source   ☐ Secondary Source

Title: _____   Author: _____

Publication Information: _____

Page(s): _____

Main Idea: _____

_____

Quotation or Paraphrase: _____

_____

Source Information   Check one: ☐ Primary Source   ☐ Secondary Source

Title: _____   Author: _____

Publication Information: _____

Page(s): _____

Main Idea: _____

_____

Quotation or Paraphrase: _____

_____

Name _____ Date _____

"Water" by Helen Keller
Take Notes for Writing to Sources

Planning Your Argument: Before you begin drafting your **argumentative essay,** use the chart below to organize your ideas. Follow the directions within each section.

1. Notes about Helen's personality and character before and after the "water" incident:	
Before the "water" incident	**After the "water" incident**
_____	_____
_____	_____
_____	_____
_____	_____
_____	_____
_____	_____
_____	_____
_____	_____
_____	_____
_____	_____

2. Notes for your introduction, in which you state your claim:

_____

_____

_____

_____

3. Notes for your point-by-point organizational structure to compare and contrast:

_____

_____

_____

_____

_____

_____

_____

4. Notes for your conclusion:

_____

_____

_____

Name _____ Date _____

Vocabulary Builder and Take Notes for Research

Academic Vocabulary

context   quotation

DIRECTIONS: *Following the directions, answer each question in a complete sentence.*

1. How is a direct *quotation* different from a description of what someone said?

_____

_____

_____

2. Explain how the *context* of an unfamiliar word can help you determine its meaning.

_____

_____

Take Notes for Research

As you research **how Winston Churchill used his determination to lead Great Britain to victory in WWII,** you can use the organizer below to take notes from your sources. As necessary, continue your notes on the back of this page, on note cards, or in a word-processing document.

Winston Churchill in WWII	
Main Idea _____ _____ Quotation or Paraphrase _____ _____ _____ _____ _____ Source Information _____ _____ _____ _____	Main Idea _____ _____ Quotation or Paraphrase _____ _____ _____ _____ _____ Source Information _____ _____ _____ _____

Unit 4: Drama
Big Question Vocabulary—1

The Big Question: How do we decide who we are?

Part of who we are has to do with other people. Other people see us a certain way because of what we choose to show them.

appearance: the way someone looks to other people

custom: something shared by people of the same culture, like a ritual or ceremony

diverse: not similar; varied

expectations: what a person thinks or hopes will happen

similar: closely the same

DIRECTIONS: *Pick any group that you are a member of, such as your class at school, a youth group, a sports team, or a group of friends. Answer the following questions about how you fit into the community you chose. Use all five vocabulary words in your answers.*

2. How are you the same as others in the group?

3. How are you different from others in the group?

1. Describe the group:

4. What kinds of things are you supposed to do as a group member?

5. What does the group do together?

Unit 4: Drama
Big Question Vocabulary—2

The Big Question: How do we decide who we are?

People are happiest when they can express who they are without worrying about what others will think.

conscious: awake; aware of what is going on

individuality: the quality that makes someone or something different from others

perspective: a personal way of thinking about something

trend: a way of doing something or thinking that is fashionable

unique: one of a kind

DIRECTIONS: *Read the passage. Then, answer the question below. Use the vocabulary words in parentheses for your responses.*

"Nobody plays board games anymore!" Clifford said to Mark. Mark's room was full of board games. It was his favorite thing to do. Mark was not sure what to say. His thoughts were going in two different directions. Should he stand up for himself or pretend to agree with Clifford? What is Mark thinking?

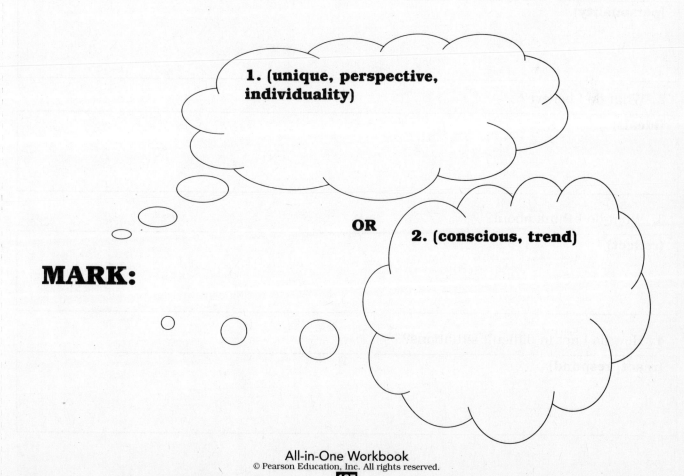

1. (unique, perspective, individuality)

OR

2. (conscious, trend)

MARK:

Name _____ Date _____

Unit 4: Drama
Big Question Vocabulary—3

The Big Question: How do we decide who we are?

Often you show your values and beliefs to others by the way you act, but sometimes your actions do not reveal your deeper feelings.

ideals: someone's ethics and beliefs

personality: a person's character, particularly the way he or she behaves toward others

reaction: action in response to an event or influence

reflect: to think back about something's value or importance

respond: to react to something that has been done or said

DIRECTIONS: *Fill in the boxes below to answer the questions. Use the vocabulary words in parentheses.*

Who am I?

1. How do I behave?

(personality)

2. What do I believe?

(ideals)

3. What do I think about?

(reflect)

4. How do I act in difficult situations?

(react, respond)

Name _____ Date _____

Unit 4: Drama
Applying the Big Question

How do we decide who we are?

DIRECTIONS: *Complete the chart below to apply what you have learned about how we decide who we are. One row has been completed for you.*

Example	Event or situation	What it shows about a person or character	What the person or character learns about himself or herself	What I learned
From Literature	In *The Phantom Tollbooth*, Milo rescues Rhyme and Reason.	Milo is willing to take risks.	He learns that he is reliable and courageous.	Solving a difficult problem can reveal our strengths.
From Literature				
From Science				
From Social Studies				
From Real Life				

Name _____ Date _____

The Phantom Tollbooth, *Act I*, based on the book by Norton Juster, by Susan Nanus

Writing About the Big Question

How do we decide who we are?

Big Question Vocabulary

appearance	conscious	custom	diverse	expectations
ideals	individuality	personality	perspective	reaction
reflect	respond	similar	trend	unique

A. *Use one or more words from the list above to complete each sentence.*

1. You can get clues to help you decide who you are in many _____ ways.

2. How you _____ to others is one way.

3. Your _____ to different kinds of people tells a great deal about you.

4. Another clue to who you are is your _____ on important issues.

5. All the special qualities that make you different from others make up your _____ _____.

B. *Follow the directions in responding to each of the items below.*

1. In two sentences, tell how you feel about two important issues in your school.

   _____

   _____

2. Write two sentences explaining why you feel the way you do about one of the preceding issues. Use at least two of the Big Question vocabulary words.

   _____

   _____

C. *In* The Phantom Tollbooth, *Act I, we meet Milo, a bored and unmotivated boy who receives an unexpected gift that leads him to take an amazing trip and to discover an adventurous side of himself. Complete the sentences below. Then, write a short paragraph in which you connect one of your answers to the Big Question.*

Boredom can often be overcome if there is a **conscious** _____

In order to discover our **individuality**, we can _____

_____

_____

_____

The Phantom Tollbooth, *Act I*, based on the book by Norton Juster, by Susan Nanus
Reading: Identify Main Events to Summarize

A **summary** of a piece of writing is a short statement that presents the main ideas and most important points. To summarize a drama, first **reread to identify main events.** Your summary should include only major events that move the story forward. Then, organize events in the order in which they happen.

DIRECTIONS: *As you read, use the road map below to record the major events in Act I of The Phantom Tollbooth. Write important information about the events in the signposts. Some of the signs have been filled in for you.*

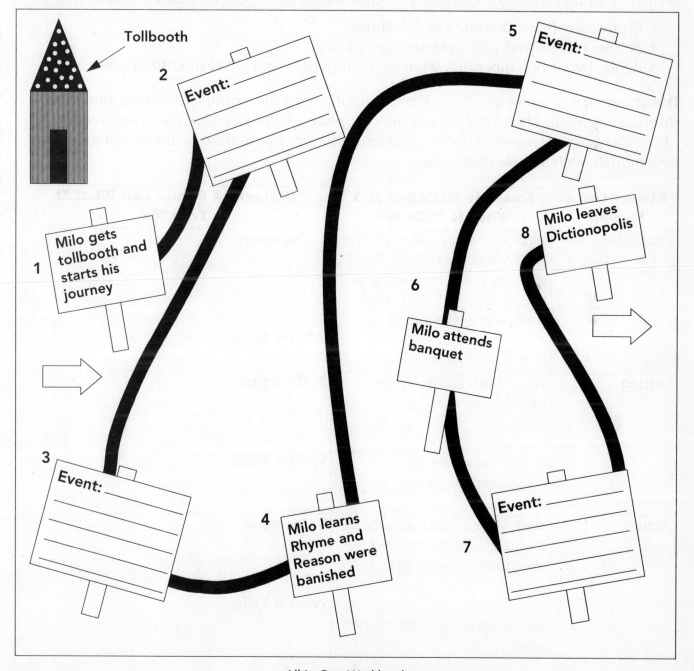

Tollbooth

5 Event: _____

2 Event: _____

1 Milo gets tollbooth and starts his journey

8 Milo leaves Dictionopolis

6 Milo attends banquet

3 Event: _____

4 Milo learns Rhyme and Reason were banished

7 Event: _____

Name _____ Date _____

The Phantom Tollbooth, Act I, based on the book by Norton Juster, by Susan Nanus
Literary Analysis: Dialogue

A *drama* is a story that is written to be performed. Like short stories, dramas have characters, a setting, and a plot. In a drama, these elements are developed mainly through **dialogue,** the words spoken by the characters. When you read the script, or written form, of a drama, the characters' names appear before their dialogue.

MILO. I'm thinking as hard as I can.

WATCHDOG. Well, think just a little harder than that. Come on, you can do it.

Paying attention to what the characters say will help you understand and enjoy the script of a drama. Dialogue can give you information about these elements in a drama:

- *Characters* (their thoughts and feelings)
- *Setting* (where and when events take place)
- *Action* (what is happening, what has happened, and what might happen)

DIRECTIONS: *Complete the chart. First, carefully read the example dialogue for each dramatic element. Then, find in Act I another piece of dialogue that gives information about that same element. Write the dialogue you find in the third column, and tell what information each sample gives you.*

Element of a Drama	Example Dialogue and What It Tells Me	Dialogue I Found and What It Tells Me
Character	MILO. Your Highness, my name is Milo and this is Tock. Thank you very much for inviting us to your banquet, and I think your palace is beautiful! (It tells me that Milo is polite.)	1. Dialogue: What It Tells:
Setting	WATCHDOG. Dictionopolis, here we come. (It tells me where the characters will go next.)	2. Dialogue: What It Tells:
Action	MILO. Why doesn't somebody rescue the Princesses and set everything straight again? (It tells me what might happen later.)	3. Dialogue What It Tells:

Name _____ Date _____

The Phantom Tollbooth, *Act I,* based on the book by Norman Juster, by Susan Nanus
Vocabulary Builder

Word List

ferocious   ignorance   misapprehension   precautionary   unabridged   unethical

A. DIRECTIONS: *For each item, write a sentence following the instructions given. Be sure that you use the underlined Word List word correctly and that your sentence expresses the meaning of the word.*

1. Use <u>precautionary</u> in a sentence about preparing for a big storm.

_____

_____

2. Use <u>ferocious</u> in a sentence about animals in the wild.

_____

_____

3. Use <u>misapprehension</u> in a sentence about exercise.

_____

_____

4. Use <u>ignorance</u> in a sentence about a test.

_____

_____

5. Use <u>unabridged</u> in a sentence about a book.

_____

_____

6. Use <u>unethical</u> in a sentence about a thief.

_____

_____

B. WORD STUDY: The root *-eth-* means "character" or "custom." Answer each of the following questions using one of these words containing *-eth-*: *ethics, unethical.*

1. Why would someone study *ethics*?

_____

2. What might be considered *unethical* behavior by a doctor?

_____

All-in-One Workbook
193

The Phantom Tollbooth, *Act I*, based on the book by Norton Juster, by Susan Nanus
Conventions: Prepositions and Appositives

A **preposition** relates a noun or pronoun to another word in the sentence. Some common prepositions include *on, with, by,* and *from.* A **prepositional phrase** begins with a preposition and includes a noun or pronoun called the **object of the preposition.**

An **appositive** is a noun or pronoun that identifies or explains another noun or pronoun in the sentence. An **appositive phrase** is a noun or pronoun with modifiers that identifies or explains another noun or pronoun in the sentence.

Preposition/ **Prepositional Phrase**	*Appositive/***Appositive Phrase**
Milo begins his journey *to* Dictionopolis. [*Dictionopolis* is the object of the preposition.]	Milo, <u>a young *boy*</u>, takes time for granted. [The phrase explains *Milo.*]
He travels *with* brave Tock. [*Tock* is the object of the preposition.]	Tock, <u>a loyal *clock*</u>, helps him. [The phrase explains *Tock.*]

A. PRACTICE: *Underline the prepositonal phrase in each sentence. Draw a circle around the object of the preposition.*

1. Milo will face many dangers on his journey.

2. Azaz gives Milo a box of letters.

B. PRACTICE: *Underline the appositive phrase in each sentence. Draw a circle around the noun or pronoun it identifies or explains.*

1. The spelling bee, a large colorful bee, can spell anything.

2. Humbug, a funny character, has trouble telling the truth.

C. Writing Application: *Write four sentences that tell about any of the events in* The Phantom Tollbooth, Act I. *For the first two sentences, use a prepositional phrase in each sentence. Underline each prepositional phrase that you use. For the last two sentences, use an appositive phrase in each sentence. Underline each appositive phrase that you use.*

1. _____

2. _____

3. _____

4. _____

Name _____   Date _____

The Phantom Tollbooth, *Act I,* based on the book by Norton Juster, by Susan Nanus
Support for Writing to Sources: Summary

A **summary** should include only the most important events, characters, and ideas in a story. Use this chart to prepare to write a summary of Act I of *The Phantom Tollbooth.* In the left-hand column, list the important events that you recorded on your earlier chart or your road map. Make sure you list the events in the order that they occurred. Then, in the right-hand column, add details about the events. For example, you might add that Rhyme and Reason are princesses who try to make peace by saying that words and numbers are equally important. Add words such as *first, then,* and *next* to make the order of events clear.

Events in Order	Details
1.	
2.	
3.	
4.	
5.	
6.	
7.	
8.	

Now, use the events and details you have listed to write your summary.

Name _____ Date _____

The Phantom Tollbooth, *Act I,* based on the book by Norton Juster, by Susan Nanus
Support for Research and Technology: Multimedia Presentation

Use the chart to record information as you gather facts about **drama** for your multimedia presentation. The categories may provide good starting points for your research.

	Source
Topic	
Illustrations	
Other Graphics	
Audio Aids	
Video Aids	

The Phantom Tollbooth, *Act II,* based on the book by Norman Juster, by Susan Nanus

Writing About the Big Question

How do we decide who we are?

Big Question Vocabulary

appearance	conscious	custom	diverse	expectations
individuality	personality	perspective	reaction	reflect
respond	similar	trend	unique	ideals

A. *Use one or more words from the list above to complete each sentence.*

1. Ana and her friend Sarah are _____ in many ways.

2. For example, they both follow the latest fashion _____.

3. However, each girl is _____ in her own way.

4. Ana likes to take time to _____ before making a decision.

5. Sarah shows her _____ by making snap decisions without giving them a second thought.

B. *Follow the directions in responding to each of the items below.*

1. In two sentences, tell two ways that you are different from your friends.

_____

_____

2. Write two sentences explaining one of the differences above and what it tells about you. Use at least two of the Big Question vocabulary words.

_____

_____

C. *In* The Phantom Tollbooth, *Act II, Milo comes back from his adventure and finds that he is interested in all of the things in his room which bored him previously. Complete the sentences below. Then, write a short paragraph in which you connect one of your answers to the Big Question.*

New experiences can give us a new **perspective** on _____

_____

In **response** to a new experience, people can develop _____

_____

_____

_____

Name _____ Date _____

The Phantom Tollbooth, *Act II*, based on the book by Norman Juster, by Susan Nanus
Reading: Picture the Action to Compare and Contrast

When you **compare** two things, you tell how they are alike. When you **contrast** two things, you tell how they are different. As you read drama, **picture the action** to compare and contrast characters, situations, and events in the play. To picture the action, pay attention to the dialogue and the descriptions of how characters speak and act.

DIRECTIONS: *Use details from Act II to compare and contrast the following pairs of characters.*

DISCHORD

1. Doctor of noise
2. _____
   _____
3. _____
   _____

BOTH

1. Are met by Milo outside Digitopolis
2. _____
   _____
3. _____
   _____

DODECAHEDRON

1. A shape with 12 faces
2. _____
   _____
3. _____
   _____

AZAZ

1. King of Dictionopolis
2. _____
   _____
3. _____
   _____

BOTH

1. Never agree
2. _____
   _____
3. _____
   _____

MATHEMAGICIAN

1. Owns a number mine
2. _____
   _____
3. _____
   _____

Name _____ Date _____

The Phantom Tollbooth, *Act II,* based on the book by Norman Juster, by Susan Nanus
Literary Analysis: Stage Directions

Stage directions are the words in a drama that the characters do not say. They tell performers how to move and speak, and they help readers picture the action, sounds, costumes, props, lighting, setting, and scenery. Stage directions are usually printed in italics and set between brackets, as in this example.

MILO. [*Timidly.*] Are you a doctor?

DISCHORD. [VOICE.] I am KAKAFONOUS A. DISCHORD, DOCTOR OF DISSONANCE!

[*Several small explosions and a grinding crash are heard.*]

Stage directions tell the actor who plays Milo to speak as if he is frightened. The stage directions following Dischord's first speech reveal the meaning of *dissonance,* an unpleasant noise.

DIRECTIONS: *Read each piece of dialogue with stage directions in the left-hand column. Then, follow the instructions or answer the questions in the right-hand column.*

Stage Direction	Information
DODECAHEDRON. We're here. This is the numbers mine. [*LIGHTS UP A LITTLE, revealing Little Men digging and chopping, shoveling and scraping.*] Right this way and watch your step. [*His voice echoes and reverberates. Iridescent and glittery numbers seem to sparkle from everywhere.*]	**1.** Underline the stage directions that make the numbers seem like jewels. **2.** The stage directions call for turning the lights up a little (from very dim light). What effect would this change have on the audience? _____ _____
MILO. But . . . what bothers me is . . . well, why is it that even when things are correct, they don't really seem to be right? MATHEMAGICIAN. [*Grows sad and quiet.*] How true. It's been that way ever since Rhyme and Reason were banished. [*Sadness turns to fury.*] And all because of that stubborn wretch Azaz! It's all his fault.	**3.** What two different feelings does the Mathemagician show here? _____ _____
MILO. Boy, I must have been gone for an awful long time. I wonder what time it is. [*Looks at clock.*] Five o'clock. I wonder what day it is. [*Looks at calendar.*] It's still today! I've been gone for an hour! [*He continues to look at calendar, and then begins to look at his books and toys and maps and chemistry set with great interest.*]	**4.** Circle the two most important props listed in these stage directions. **5.** What change in Milo do the stage directions reveal? _____ _____ _____

The Phantom Tollbooth, *Act II,* based on the book by Norman Juster, by Susan Nanus
Vocabulary Builder

Word List

admonishing   deficiency   dissonance   iridescent   malicious   transfixed

A. DIRECTIONS: *Based on the instructions given, write sentences that use the Word List words correctly and express the meanings of the words.*

1. Write a sentence about a coach speaking to players who are not paying attention. Use *admonishing* and *deficiency.*

   _____

   _____

2. Write a sentence about the way a brightly colored but noisy bird looks and sounds. Use *iridescent* and *dissonance.*

   _____

   _____

3. Write a sentence about a snowball fight. Use *transfixed* and *malicious.*

   _____

   _____

B. WORD STUDY: The prefix *trans-* means "across" or "through." Answer each of the following questions using one of these words containing *trans-: transcends, transfixed, translation, transparent.*

1. What are two items that are *transparent?*

   _____

2. Why would you need a *translation* of a book?

   _____

3. What might cause a deer to be *transfixed?*

   _____

4. What kind of story *transcends* belief?

   _____

Name _____ Date _____

The Phantom Tollbooth, Act II, based on the book by Norton Just...

Conventions: Participles and Gerund. Susan Nanus

Present and Past Participles and Participial Phrases

A **participle** is a verb form that acts as an adjective. A **present partici**...
A **past participle** usually ends in -ed. However, past participles of irregu... in -ing.
differently—for example, *caught, hidden, cut.* A **participial phrase** contai...s end
present participle along with other words to make a phrase. ...st or

Present participles:	Laughing, he ran to the sparkling river.
Past participles:	Frightened, they ran from the smoke-filled room.
Participial phrases:	*Benched by her coach* and *sulking in the dugout,* the playe...

Gerunds and Gerund Phrases

A **gerund** is a verb form that ends in -ing and is used as a noun. A **gerund phrase**
group of words containing a gerund and any modifiers or other words that relate to...

Gerund:	Dancing is fun.	I enjoy skating.
Gerund phrase:	Dancing with you is fun.	I enjoy skating in the park.

A. PRACTICE: *Underline the participle or participial phrase or the gerund or gerund phrase in each sentence.*

1. Please make that dog stop its barking.

2. Reading a text message, Logan began to laugh.

3. Well-trained for the marathon, the runners gathered near the START banner.

4. For the party, we tried making individual pizzas.

5. Playing guitar and bass, the musician hoped to join a band.

6. Running, walking, and swimming are good ways to exercise.

7. We listened to the howling of wolves in the distance.

8. Exhausted from the long hike, we fell onto our cots.

B. WRITING APPLICATION: *Write about some of the things you do during summer vacation. Include and underline participles or participial phrases and gerunds or gerund phrases in four of the sentences. Identify the participles and gerunds by writing a P or G above each.*

_____

_____

_____

_____

Name _____ Date _____

The Phantom To... th, *Act II,* based on the book by Norman Juster, by Susan Nanus

port for **Writing to Sources: Review**

Use this pa... ...ake notes for your **review** of *The Phantom Tollbooth*. Remember
that you are ...ng the entire play, not just Act II.

...state your overall opinion; be sure to include the title and author of

1. **Introd**...
   the w..._____

   _____

   _____

   ...**ked** (include reasons and supporting details):

   2_____

   _____

   _____

   ...ts I disliked (include reasons and supporting details):

   _____

   _____

   _____

4. **Characters I liked most** (and why):

   _____

   _____

   _____

5. **Characters I liked least** (and why):

   _____

   _____

   _____

6. **Conclusion** (end with strong and interesting sentences that summarize your overall opinion):

   _____

   _____

   _____

Now, use the opinions and examples you have listed to write your review.

The Phantom Tollbooth, *Act II*, based on the book by Norman Juster, by Susan Nanus
Support for Speaking and Listening: Group Discussion

Use the following questions to guide your group discussion about how reading the play was similar to and different from listening to it. Explain your answers.

1. Did hearing different characters' voices make the play easier to understand?

   _____

   _____

   _____

   _____

2. Was hearing speakers emphasize certain words helpful? Did you mentally emphasize the same words as you read?

   _____

   _____

   _____

   _____

3. Did listening to the play or reading the play make it easier to imagine the action?

   _____

   _____

   _____

   _____

4. Which of your classmates' claims about listening versus reading the play were supported with strong evidence or reasons?

   _____

   _____

   _____

   _____

from **You're a Good Man, Charlie Brown** by Clark Gesner
"Happiness Is a Charming Charlie Brown at Orlando Rep" by Matthew MacDermid
Writing About the Big Question

How do we decide who we are?

Big Question Vocabulary

appearance	conscious	custom	diverse	expectations
ideals	individuality	personality	perspective	reaction
reflect	respond	similar	trend	unique

A. *Use one or more words from the list above to complete each sentence.*

1. It is the _____ of some people to make snap judgments about others.

2. People cannot tell what you are really like by just looking at your outward _____ _____.

3. They should make a _____ effort to get to know what you are like on the inside.

4. In any case, you should not try to live up to others' _____ of you.

5. Always be true to your own set of _____.

B. *Follow the directions in responding to each of the items below.*

1. In two sentences, give two instances when your first impression of someone turned out to be wrong.

   _____

   _____

2. Write two sentences explaining one of the instances above and what it taught you. Use at least two of the Big Question vocabulary words.

   _____

   _____

   _____

C. *In the drama you will read, Lucy asks questions to find out more about herself. In the nonfiction article, the author discusses how the actors embody the characters they play. How does an actor decide who a character is? Complete the sentence below. Then, write a short paragraph in which you connect this idea to the Big Question.*

To play a character successfully, an actor needs to understand certain things about the character, such as _____

_____

_____

from **You're a Good Man, Charlie Brown** by Clark Gesner
"Happiness Is a Charming Charlie Brown at Orlando Rep" by Matthew MacDermid
Literary Analysis: Author's Purpose in Drama and Nonfiction

The **author's purpose** is the main reason the author writes a work. The types of details used in the work suggest the purpose. An author might have many different reasons for writing, such as

- to entertain
- to explain a process
- to persuade
- to inform
- to share an opinion

A. DIRECTIONS: *Read each passage, and answer the questions that follow.*

from **You're a Good Man, Charlie Brown by Clark Gesner**

LUCY. Come on, Linus, answer the question.

LINUS. *(Getting up and facing LUCY)* Look, Lucy, I know very well that if I give any sort of honest answer to that question you're going to slug me.

LUCY. Linus. A survey that is not based on honest answers is like a house that is built on a foundation of sand. Would I be spending my time to conduct this survey if I didn't expect complete candor in all the responses? I promise not to slug you. Now what number would you give me as your crabbiness rating?

LINUS. *(After a few moments of interior struggle)* Ninety-five. *(LUCY sends a straight jab to his jaw which lays him out flat)*

LUCY. No decent person could be expected to keep her word with a rating over ninety. *(She stalks off, busily figuring away on her clipboard)*. . .

1. What types of details does the author use?

   _____

2. What is the author's purpose? _____

from **"Happiness Is a Charming Charlie Brown at Orlando Rep" by Matthew MacDermid**

However, three performers take their characters to a higher level, stealing the spotlight with every opportunity and even chewing a bit of the scenery along the way. Shannon Bilo is a wonder as Lucy, with a clarion belt and expert comic timing that seem to go for days. Mark Catlett is outstanding as her kid brother Linus, sucking his thumb and doing the tango with his blanket, all the while exuding the mind-numbing intelligence of such a youngster. . . .

3. What types of details does the author use?

   _____

4. What is the author's purpose? _____

from **You're a Good Man, Charlie Brown** by Clark Gesner
"Happiness Is a Charming Charlie Brown at Orlando Rep" by Matthew MacDermid
Vocabulary Builder

Word List

> abundantly   civic   evoking   embody   objectionable   tentatively

A. DIRECTIONS: Provide an answer and an explanation for each question.

1. If you *tentatively* answer a question, how sure are you about your answer?

   _____

2. If someone acts in an *objectionable* way at a party, would the host be likely to invite that person to his next party?

   _____

3. If you find a lesson to be *abundantly* clear, how much help would you need to understand the material?

   _____

4. If a movie is *evoking* laughter, what kind of movie is it?

   _____

5. If you see objects that *embody* the ideas of an architect, what are you viewing?

   _____

6. If you have *civic* duties, can you be a recluse?

   _____

B. DIRECTIONS: *Circle the letter of the word that is most nearly opposite in meaning to the word in CAPITAL letters.*

____ 1. OBJECTIONABLE:
         A. cautious   B. clever   C. cruel   D. pleasant

____ 2. TENTATIVELY:
         A. kindly   B. boldly   C. finally   D. justly

____ 3. ABUNDANTLY:
         A. seriously   B. orderly   C. somewhat   D. readily

____ 4. CIVIC:
         A. private   B. biased   C. specific   D. illegal

from You're a Good Man, Charlie Brown by Clark Gesner
"Happiness Is a Charming Charlie Brown at Orlando Rep" by Matthew MacDermid
Support for Writing to Compare Author's Purpose

Before you draft your essay comparing and contrasting each author's purpose for writing, complete the graphic organizers below.

Story told by fictitious characters	Selection Title:
Which details create humor?	
Which details suggest a lesson to be learned?	

Contains author's thoughts and feelings	Selection Title:
What does he praise?	
What does he criticize?	
What is his overall point of view?	

Now use your notes to write an essay comparing and contrasting each author's purpose for writing.

Writing Process
Problem-and-Solution Essay

Prewriting: Gathering Details

Use the chart provided to begin gathering information for your problem-and-solution essay. The first column will include details that clearly explain the problem. The second column will have details that show why and how your solution will work.

Problem	Why and how the solution will work

Drafting: Using an Organizational Plan

Use the following graphic organizer to organize your essay.

Introduction including thesis

↓

Explanation of problem

↓

Step-by-step description of solution

↓

Evidence supporting solution

↓

Conclusion

Writer's Toolbox
Conventions: Sentence Variety

You can add **variety to your sentence patterns** and pack in information by using prepositional phrases, appositive phrases, participial phrases, or gerund phrases. Here are some examples:

Example: The snow fell softly. The village was quiet.
Combined with a prepositional phrase (as an adverb): The snow fell softly *on the quiet village*.
Example: Jaime is a video-game expert. He wins all his games.
Combined with an appositive phrase: Jaime, *a video-game expert*, wins all his games.

Example: The book was fascinating. Kate finished it in two days.
Combined with a participial phrase: *Fascinated by the book*, Kate finished it in two days.

Example: You are eating too much pudding. It will make you sick.
Combined with a gerund phrase: *Eating too much pudding* will make you sick.

A. PRACTICE: *Underline the phrase in each sentence. Then, use the line provided to write the type of the phrase:* prepositional, participial, appositive, *or* gerund.

_____ 1. Hitting an icy patch is a danger for drivers.

_____ 2. The team, a state championship winner, is doing even better this year.

_____ 3. At the school day's end, teachers finally get a rest.

_____ 4. Standing excitedly, Jonathan cheered the runners.

B. WRITING APPLICATION: *Combine the following sentences using phrases.*

1. Lucy likes to sing in the choir. Lucy is a talented performer.

_____

2. Harold walked slowly. The sidewalk was icy.

_____

3. Do not exercise in this heat. It will give you heatstroke.

_____

4. The fans stood during the final minutes of the game. They cheered when their team won.

_____

Name _____ Date _____

The Prince and the Pauper, adapted from the play and the book by Mark Twain
Vocabulary Builder

Selection Vocabulary

affliction   pauper   sauntered

A. DIRECTIONS: *For each item below, follow the instructions and write a sentence. Be sure that you use the italicized word correctly and that your sentence expresses the meaning of each word.*

1. Use *affliction* in a sentence about someone who suffers from a skin rash.

   _____

2. Use *sauntered* in a sentence about walking around in your neighborhood.

   _____

3. Use *pauper* in a sentence about a fictional child who is an orphan.

   _____

Academic Vocabulary

respond   similar   technique

B. DIRECTIONS: *Create two different sentences for each of the following words. Try to use the word to explain something entirely different in your second sentence.*

Example: The baseball player was <u>exhausted</u> after the game went into extra innings. After the manager had <u>exhausted</u> the entire list of alternates, he began looking for other players to complete the team.

RESPOND

1. _____

2. _____

SIMILAR

3. _____

4. _____

TECHNIQUE

5. _____

6. _____

Name _____ Date _____

The Prince and the Pauper, adapted from the play and the book by Mark Twain
Take Notes for Discussion

Before the Partner Discussion: Read the passage from the selection in your textbook.

PRINCE. *(Violently)* King? What King, good sir?

1ST PRISONER. Why, we only have one, his most sacred majesty, King Edward the Sixth.

2ND PRISONER. And whether he be mad or not, his praises are on all men's lips. He has saved many innocent lives, and now he means to destroy the cruelest laws that oppress the people.

PRINCE. *(Turning away, shaking his head)* How can this be? Surely it is not that little beggar boy!

During the Discussion: As you and your partner discuss each question, take notes on how your partners' ideas either differ from or build upon your own.

Discussion Questions	Other Responses	Comparison to My Responses
1. What does this passage suggest about the real qualifications of a king?		
2. What does the Prince's surprise imply about differences between Tom and himself?		

Name _____   Date _____

The Prince and the Pauper, adapted from the play and the book by Mark Twain
Take Notes for Writing to Sources

Planning Your Informative Text: Before you begin drafting your **comparison-and-contrast essay,** use the diagram below to organize your ideas. Compare the two characters on the following points: **personality, behavior, motivation.**

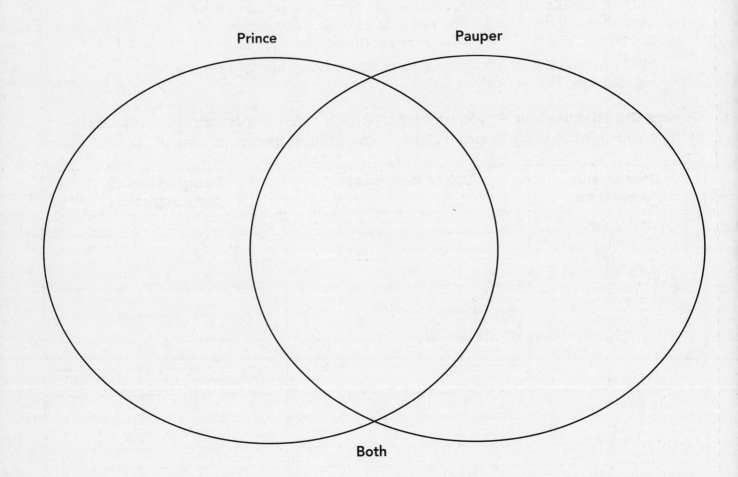

Prince

Pauper

Both

Name _____ Date _____

The Prince and the Pauper, adapted from the play and the book by Mark Twain
Take Notes for Research

As you research **to learn about the Palace of Westminster and its long history,** use the forms below to take notes from your sources. As necessary, continue your notes on the back of this page, on note cards, or in a word-processing document.

Source Information   Check one: ☐ Primary Source   ☐ Secondary Source

Title: _____   Author: _____

Publication Information: _____

Page(s): _____

Main Idea: _____

_____

Quotation or Paraphrase: _____

_____

Source Information   Check one: ☐ Primary Source   ☐ Secondary Source

Title: _____   Author: _____

Publication Information: _____

Page(s): _____

Main Idea: _____

_____

Quotation or Paraphrase: _____

_____

Source Information   Check one: ☐ Primary Source   ☐ Secondary Source

Title: _____   Author: _____

Publication Information: _____

Page(s): _____

Main Idea: _____

_____

Quotation or Paraphrase: _____

_____

Name _____ Date _____

Vocabulary Builder

Selection Vocabulary

agonizing   awed   compulsion

A. DIRECTIONS: *For each item below, follow the instructions and write a sentence. Be sure that you use the italicized word correctly and that your sentence expresses the meaning of each word.*

1. Use *compulsion* in a sentence about people who participate in a dangerous sport.

   _____

2. Use *awed* in a sentence about a tornado.

   _____

3. Use *agonizing* in a sentence about a difficult decision a person might have to make.

   _____

Academic Vocabulary

common   opinion   purpose

B. DIRECTIONS: *Write a response to each question. Make sure to use the italicized word at least once in your response.*

1. What is a *common* sight that you see every day?

   _____

2. What is your *opinion* on the value of recycling plastic bottles?

   _____

3. What do you think is an important *purpose* in writing poetry?

   _____

Name _____   Date _____

"Stage Fright" by Mark Twain
Take Notes for Discussion

Before the Panel Discussion: Read the following passage from the selection.

> At last I began. I had the manuscript tucked under a United States
> flag in front of me where I could get at it in case of need. But I
> managed to get started without it.

During the Discussion: As the panel discusses each question, take notes on how other students' ideas either differ from or build upon your own.

Discussion Questions	Other Ideas Expressed	Comparison to My Own Ideas
1. What is Twain worried about?		
2. For what purpose does he put the manuscript under a U.S. flag? Why is that funny?		

Name _____ Date _____

"Stage Fright" by Mark Twain
Take Notes for Research

As you research **more about stage fright,** use the chart below to take notes from your sources. As necessary, continue your notes on the back of this page, on note cards, or in a word-processing document.

Source Information   Check one: ☐ Primary Source   ☐ Secondary Source

Title: _____   Author: _____

Publication Information: _____

Page(s): _____

Main Idea: _____

_____

Quotation or Paraphrase: _____

_____

Source Information   Check one: ☐ Primary Source   ☐ Secondary Source

Title: _____   Author: _____

Publication Information: _____

Page(s): _____

Main Idea: _____

_____

Quotation or Paraphrase: _____

_____

Source Information   Check one: ☐ Primary Source   ☐ Secondary Source

Title: _____   Author: _____

Publication Information: _____

Page(s): _____

Main Idea: _____

_____

Quotation or Paraphrase: _____

_____

All-in-One Workbook
216

"Stage Fright" by Mark Twain
Take Notes for Writing to Sources

Planning Your Informative Text: Before you begin drafting your **how-to essay,** use the chart below to organize your ideas.

---

1. Topic:

_____

_____

2. Organization of your ideas:

_____

_____

_____

_____

_____

_____

_____

_____

3. Details about your topic:

_____

_____

_____

_____

_____

_____

_____

4. Transitions that will show the relationships among ideas:

_____

_____

_____

_____

Name _____ Date _____

"My Papa, Mark Twain" by Susy Clemens
Vocabulary Builder

Selection Vocabulary

consequently   incessantly   striking

A. DIRECTIONS: *For each item below, follow the instructions and write a sentence. Be sure that you use the vocabulary words correctly and that your sentence expresses the meaning of each word.*

1. Use *consequently* in a sentence about homework.

   _____

   _____

2. Use *striking* and *incessantly* in a sentence about a fireworks display.

   _____

   _____

Academic Vocabulary

convincing   credible   identify

B. DIRECTIONS: *Write two different sentences for each of the following words. You may use different forms of the vocabulary word for your second sentence.*

   Example: The committee chairperson was difficult and <u>controlling</u>.
   She maintained tight <u>control</u> over the discussions.

1. **convincing:** _____

   _____

2. **credible:** _____

   _____

3. **identify:** _____

   _____

Name _____ Date _____

"My Papa, Mark Twain" by Susy Clemens
Take Notes for Discussion

Before the Partner Discussion: Read the following passage from the selection.

I never saw a man with so much variety of feeling as papa has; now the "Prince and the Pauper" is full of touching places, but there is always a streak of humor in them somewhere. Papa very seldom writes a passage without some humor in it somewhere and I don't think he ever will.

During the Discussion: As you discuss each question, take notes on how your partner's ideas either differ from or build upon your own.

Discussion Questions	Other Ideas Expressed	Comparison to My Own Ideas
1. How is this passage typical of the entire biography?		
2. How is Susy Clemens like a traditional biographer? How is she different?		

Name _____ Date _____

As you research the **biography of Mark Twain and compare the biographer's portrayal of Twain with Susy Clemens's portrayal,** you can use the forms below. As necessary, continue your notes on the back of this page, on note cards, or in a word-processing document.

Mark Twain	
Main Idea _____ _____	Main Idea _____ _____
Quotation or Paraphrase _____ _____ _____ _____	Quotation or Paraphrase _____ _____ _____ _____
Source Information _____ _____ _____ _____	Source Information _____ _____ _____ _____
Main Idea _____ _____	Main Idea _____ _____
Quotation or Paraphrase _____ _____ _____ _____	Quotation or Paraphrase _____ _____ _____ _____
Source Information _____ _____ _____ _____	Source Information _____ _____ _____ _____

Name _____ Date _____

"My Papa, Mark Twain" by Susy Clemens
Take Notes for Writing to Sources

Planning Your Argument: Before you begin drafting your **argument,** use the chart below to organize your ideas.

1. Notes for introducing your claim:

_____
_____

2. Evidence from "My Papa, Mark Twain" to support your claim:

_____
_____
_____
_____
_____
_____
_____

3. Your consideration of opposing views:

_____
_____
_____
_____
_____
_____
_____
_____

4. Notes for your conclusion:

_____
_____
_____
_____
_____

"Mark Twain's First 'Vacation,'" from *The New York World*
Vocabulary Builder

Selection Vocabulary

deliberate   distinctly   vigor

A. DIRECTIONS: *Write at least one synonym, one antonym, and an example sentence for each word. Synonyms and antonyms can be words or phrases.*

Word	Synonym	Antonym	Example Sentence
deliberate			
distinctly			
vigor			

Academic Vocabulary

achieve   conflict   retells

B. DIRECTIONS: *Answer each question. Write your response in a full sentence.*

1. What is one thing you would like to *achieve* during your lifetime?

   _____

2. Why might two nations have a *conflict*?

   _____

3. How might a present-day writer change an old folk tale or fable when he or she *retells* it?

   _____

Name _____ Date _____

"Mark Twain's First 'Vacation,'" from *The New York World*
Take Notes for Discussion

Before the Group Discussion: Read the following passage from the selection.

> Well, it kept on raining and storming generally until toward evening, when, seventeen miles below Hannibal, I was discovered by one of the crew." A very deliberate pause.
>
> "They put me ashore at Louisiana." Another pause.
>
> "I was sent home by some friends of my father's. My father met me on my return." A twinkle in the steel-blue eyes. "I remember that quite distinctly."

During the Discussion: As your group discusses each question, take notes on how other students' ideas either differ from or build upon your own.

Discussion Questions	Other Ideas Expressed	Comparison to My Own Ideas
1. What details does the interviewer add to the text? What effect do these details achieve?		
2. How is the format of this interview different from other interviews you have read?		

Name _____ Date _____

"Mark Twain's First 'Vacation,'" from *The New York World*
Take Notes for Research

As you research **riverboats on the Mississippi River before the Civil War,** you can use the forms below. As necessary, continue your notes on the back of this page, on note cards, or in a word-processing document.

Source Information Check one: ☐ Primary Source ☐ Secondary Source

Title: _____ Author: _____

Publication Information: _____

Page(s): _____

Main Idea: _____

_____

Quotation or Paraphrase: _____

_____

Source Information Check one: ☐ Primary Source ☐ Secondary Source

Title: _____ Author: _____

Publication Information: _____

Page(s): _____

Main Idea: _____

_____

Quotation or Paraphrase: _____

_____

Source Information Check one: ☐ Primary Source ☐ Secondary Source

Title: _____ Author: _____

Publication Information: _____

Page(s): _____

Main Idea: _____

_____

Quotation or Paraphrase: _____

_____

Name _____ Date _____

Take Notes for Writing to Sources

Planning Your Narrative: Before you begin drafting your **retelling,** use the chart below to organize your ideas. First, identify the character whose point of view you will use.

Character: _____

1. Details you will use in your narrative: _____ _____ _____ _____ _____ _____
2. Sequence of events: _____ _____ _____ _____ _____ _____
3. Notes about Twain's father's point of view: _____ _____ _____
4. Samples of dialogue: _____ _____
5. Notes for your conclusion: _____ _____ _____

"According to Mark Twain"
Academic Vocabulary and Take Notes for Research

establish   modify   quotation

A. DIRECTIONS: *Following the directions, answer each question in a complete sentence.*

1. Name one way you might *establish* a new friendship.

   _____

2. What school rule would you like to *modify*?

   _____

3. Why is it important to use exact words when giving a *quotation* from a speech or a piece of literature?

   _____

Take Notes for Research

As you research **additional quotations from Twain,** you can use the organizer below to take notes from your sources. As necessary, continue your notes on the back of this page, on note cards, or in a word-processing document.

Quotations of Mark Twain	
Quotation _____ _____ Source Information _____ _____	Quotation _____ _____ Source Information _____ _____
Quotation _____ _____ Source Information _____ _____	Quotation _____ _____ Source Information _____ _____
Quotation _____ Source Information _____ _____	Quotation _____ Source Information _____ _____

Name _____ Date _____

Vocabulary Builder

Selection Vocabulary

astonishing   notorious   rapture

A. DIRECTIONS: *Following the directions, answer each question in a complete sentence.*

1. Describe what you think is an *astonishing* sight in nature. _____

   _____

2. Name one *notorious* outlaw from the past. _____

   _____

3. Why might a young child respond with *rapture* on opening a birthday gift? _____

   _____

Academic Vocabulary

interviews   pose   refer

B. DIRECTIONS: *Write two different sentences for each word. You may use different forms of the vocabulary word for your second sentence.*

> **Example:** The committee chairperson was difficult and <u>controlling</u>.
> She maintained tight <u>control</u> over the discussions.

1. **interviews**

   _____

   _____

2. **pose**

   _____

   _____

3. **refer**

   _____

   _____

"An Encounter With an Interviewer" by Mark Twain
Take Notes for Discussion

Before the Small Group Discussion: Read the passage from the selection in your textbook that begins and ends as shown below.

Q. Well, I believe I have got material enough for the present . . .
I was sorry to see him go.

During the Discussion: As the group discusses each question, take notes on how other students' ideas either differ from or build upon your own.

Discussion Questions	Other Ideas Expressed	Comparison to My Own Ideas
1. Is the narrator really sorry to see the interviewer go? How can you tell?		
2. Why does the narrator pose as an unreliable interview subject?		

"An Encounter With an Interviewer" by Mark Twain
Take Notes for Research

As you research **one or more interviews that Twain gave during his lifetime,** you can use the organizer below to take notes from your sources. As necessary, continue your notes on the back of this page, on note cards, or in a word-processing document.

Interviews With Mark Twain

Main Idea _____
_____

Quotation or Paraphrase _____
_____
_____
_____
_____

Source Information _____
_____
_____
_____

Main Idea _____
_____

Quotation or Paraphrase _____
_____
_____
_____
_____

Source Information _____
_____
_____
_____

Main Idea _____
_____

Quotation or Paraphrase _____
_____
_____
_____
_____

Source Information _____
_____
_____
_____

Main Idea _____
_____

Quotation or Paraphrase _____
_____
_____
_____
_____

Source Information _____
_____
_____
_____

"An Encounter With an Interviewer" by Mark Twain
Take Notes for Writing to Sources

Planning Your Argument: Before you begin drafting your **argument,** use the chart below to organize your ideas.

1. Your claim:
2. Reasons for your claim in order of importance:
3. Evidence to support your claim:
4. Precise words that will convey your main point:
5. Notes for your conclusion:

All-in-One Workbook
230

Name _____ Date _____

Unit 5: Themes in Folk Literature
Big Question Vocabulary—1

The Big Question: How much do our communities shape us?

For many people, family is their most important community. This may include extended family—grandparents, cousins, aunts, and uncles; just immediate family—parents and siblings; or any group of people that a person lives with and has close ties to.

common: shared by all

family: a group of people who are all related and usually live together

generation: a group of people who were all born around the same time

influence: to have an effect on the way someone or something develops, behaves, or thinks without using force

support: to agree with someone else and offer your help

DIRECTIONS: *Answer the following questions using the vocabulary words in parentheses.*

1. What are the names of the people you live with? **(family)**

   _____

   _____

   _____

2. What are the ages of people in your family? How many people in your extended family are in similar age groups? **(generation)**

   _____

   _____

   _____

3. What do you share with your family? **(common)**

   _____

   _____

   _____

4. How have you helped other members of your family and/or how have they helped you? **(support)**

   _____

   _____

   _____

5. What effect do other members of your family have on you? **(influence)**

   _____

   _____

   _____

Name _____   Date _____

Unit 5: Themes in Folk Literature
Big Question Vocabulary—2

The Big Question: How much do our communities shape us?

Larger groups of people that we are associated with form our communities. They can be the people in our neighborhood, our school, a club that we belong to, or the place where we work.

belief: the feeling that something is definitely true or definitely exists

community: a group of people who live in the same area or a group of people who share a common interest

connection: a situation where two or more people understand each other

participation: taking part in an activity or event

values: a person's principles about what is right and wrong and what is important in life

Elana belongs to a youth group. She is making a brochure for new members, but she is having trouble finishing her sentences. Finish Elana's sentences for her. Include each of the above vocabulary words at least once.

Webbville Youth Group (WYG)

WYG is more than just a youth group. We are a (1) _____.
This is demonstrated by (2) _____ _____
_____.

The members of WYG share the (3) _____ that helping one another and being there for one another is (4) _____
_____.

If you decide to join WYG, you won't regret it. Your (5) _____
_____
_____.

WYG'S (6) _____
Be kind.
Be supportive of your friends.
Be polite.
Help others.

Name _____ Date _____

Unit 5: Themes in Folk Literature
Big Question Vocabulary—3

The Big Question: How much do our communities shape us?

People who share a similar background often understand each other more easily than people with diverse backgrounds. But through communication, people can learn about and feel comfortable with those from other backgrounds.

culture: ideas, beliefs, and customs that are shared by people in a society

group: several people or things that are related in some way

history: everything that has happened in the past

involve: to include something as a necessary part

isolate: to stop something or someone from having contact with particular people or ideas

Brian had just moved from a small town to a big city. He felt lonely. In his old town he shared the same ideas, beliefs, and customs as his small-town friends. Here, he didn't understand people's ideas, beliefs, and customs.

Finish the sentences below. Use the vocabulary words (or some form of each word) in parentheses

Brian told his old friend Steve,

1. "(isolate, culture)"

Steve advised Brian to find others with similar interests so that he would meet people. Steve said,

2. "(involve, group)"

Brian was grateful for Steve's advice. Brian understood him because they shared a similar past. Brian said,

3. "(history)"

Name _____ Date _____

Unit 5: Themes in Folk Literature
Applying the Big Question

 How much do our communities shape us?

DIRECTIONS: *Complete the chart below to apply what you have learned about ways that communities shape the lives of their members. One row has been completed for you.*

Example	Community	Description of this community	Problem or issue	Outcome of the problem or issue	What I learned
From Literature	characters from *Black Ships Before Troy*	ancient Greek gods and human beings	Three goddesses quarrel because each believes that she deserves to be called "the fairest."	The three goddesses ask a mortal man, Paris, to judge their contest. Paris declares Aphrodite the winner.	It is best not to take sides in private quarrels among powerful people. You may end up with powerful enemies.
From Literature					
From Science					
From Social Studies					
From Real Life					

"The Tiger Who Would Be King" by James Thurber
"The Ant and the Dove" by Leo Tolstoy
Writing About the Big Question

How much do our communities shape us?

Big Question Vocabulary

belief	common	community	connection	culture
family	generation	group	history	influence
involve	isolate	participation	support	values

A. *Use one or more words from the list above to complete each sentence.*

1. Juan enjoyed going to the town picnic because it made him feel he was part of a
   _____.

2. Every time Elizabeth played a tennis match, she had a strong _____
   that she would win.

3. David and Shauna discovered that being in the photography club had begun to
   _____ the kinds of photos they took, since they were learning from
   the other members.

4. Before Raj decided to work on the senator's re-election campaign, he checked into
   her _____, including her voting record and speeches.

B. *Follow the directions in responding to each of the items below.*

1. List two different times when being part of a group made you act in a certain way.

   _____

   _____

2. Write two sentences explaining one of the preceding experiences, and describe how
   it made you feel. Use at least two of the Big Question vocabulary words.

   _____

   _____

   _____

C. *Complete the sentence below. Then, write a short paragraph in which you connect this
experience to the Big Question.*

Members of my community helped one another when _____

   _____

   _____

   _____

   _____

"The Tiger Who Would Be King" by James Thurber
"The Ant and the Dove" by Leo Tolstoy

Reading: Reread to Analyze Cause-and-Effect Relationships

A **cause** is an event, an action, or a feeling that produces a result. The result that is produced is called an **effect.** Sometimes an effect is the result of a number of different causes. To help you identify the relationships between an event and its causes, **reread** important passages in the work, looking for connections. In some stories, all the causes (the events) lead in one way or another to the effect (how the story turns out).

You can use a chart like the one below to record events and actions that work together to produce an effect. You may need to rearrange the lines and arrows for different works. This chart shows you how causes lead to two effects in "The Tiger Who Would Be King."

DIRECTIONS: *Fill in the missing causes and effect.*

1. CAUSE: The tiger wants to be king of beasts.

   EFFECT A: The tiger challenges the lion.

2. CAUSE: _____

3. CAUSE: The lion defends his crown.

4. CAUSE: _____ → **EFFECT B:** _____

5. CAUSE: _____

"The Tiger Who Would Be King" by James Thurber
"The Ant and the Dove" by Leo Tolstoy
Literary Analysis: Fables and Folk Tales

Fables and **folk tales** are part of the oral tradition of passing songs, stories, and poems from generation to generation by word of mouth.

- **Fables** are brief stories that teach a lesson or moral. They often feature animal characters.
- **Folk tales** feature heroes, adventure, magic, and romance. These stories often entertain while teaching a lesson.

DIRECTIONS: *Read "The Tiger Who Would Be King" and "The Ant and the Dove." Answer the following items as you read.*

"The Tiger Who Would Be King"

1. Who are the main characters in this fable? _____

_____

2. Which character, if any, is someone you can admire as a hero? _____

3. Give one reason for your answer to question 2. _____

_____

4. In your own words, what is the moral or lesson of the fable? _____

_____

_____

"The Ant and the Dove"

5. Who are the main characters in this folk tale? _____

_____

6. Which character, if any, is someone you can admire as a hero? _____

7. Give one reason for your answer to question 6. _____

_____

8. What lesson about life does this folk tale teach? _____

_____

_____

"**The Tiger Who Would Be King**" by James Thurber
"**The Ant and the Dove**" by Leo Tolstoy
Vocabulary Builder

Word List

inquired   monarch   prowled   repaid   repulse   startled

A. DIRECTIONS: *Write a* **synonym** *for each vocabulary word. Use a thesaurus if you need one. Write a sentence that includes the synonym. Be sure that your sentence makes the meaning of the word clear.*

Vocabulary word: defend

Synonym: protect

Sentence: The tigress fought to <u>protect</u> her cubs during the battle.

1. Vocabulary word: **startled**   Synonym: _____

   Sentence: _____

2. Vocabulary word: **prowled**   Synonym: _____

   Sentence: _____

3. Vocabulary word: **repulse**   Synonym: _____

   Sentence: _____

4. Vocabulary word: **inquired**   Synonym: _____

   Sentence: _____

5. Vocabulary word: **monarch**   Synonym: _____

   Sentence: _____

6. Vocabulary word: **repaid**   Synonym: _____

   Sentence: _____

B. WORD STUDY: The suffix *-ment* means "the act, art, or process of." Complete each of the following sentences about a word containing *-ment*.

1. As *repayment* to a friend for a favor, you might

   _____

2. The *argument* between the two teams involved

   _____

3. The candidate gave a *statement* in which

   _____

"The Tiger Who Would Be King" by James Thurber
"The Ant and the Dove" by Leo Tolstoy
Conventions: Subject Complements

Some sentences use linking verbs such as *be, is, were, feel, appear,* or *seems.* In those sentences, the **subject complements** that complete the idea of the subject and verb are called predicate nouns or predicate adjectives. A **predicate noun** renames or identifies the subject of a sentence. A **predicate adjective** describes the subject of a sentence.

> James Thurber was an American <u>humorist</u>. (predicate noun—*identifies* the subject, James Thurber)
> Leo Tolstoy's stories are <u>timeless</u>. (predicate adjective—*describes* stories)

A. PRACTICE: *Look at the underlined subject complement in each sentence. Draw an arrow to the word or phrase that the subject complement renames or describes. Then, write whether the subject complement is a predicate noun or a predicate adjective. The first one has been done for you.*

1. The sky was <u>cloudy</u> all day. <u>predicate adjective</u>

2. Leo Tolstoy's novels are <u>famous</u> all over the world. _____

3. Sacramento is the <u>capital</u> of California. _____

4. Kira and Naomi were the highest <u>scorers</u> in the game. _____

5. A sari is the traditional outer <u>garment</u> of an Indian woman. _____

6. Commercials on television are often <u>loud</u> and <u>annoying</u>. _____

B. WRITING APPLICATION: *Write five sentences to describe a place in nature that you have seen. Use predicate nouns or predicate adjectives in your sentences. Underline and number five predicate nouns and predicate adjectives. Then, write PN or PA next to the item number below your description.*

1. _____

2. _____

3. _____

4. _____

5. _____

1. _____   2. _____   3. _____   4. _____   5. _____

"The Tiger Who Would Be King" by James Thurber
"The Ant and the Dove" by Leo Tolstoy
Support for Writing to Sources: Fable

Before you write your fable, figure out the causes and effects that lead up to the lesson of your story. Begin by writing down your story ideas on the chart below.

Lesson	
Animal characters	
Their situation or conflict	

Next, decide on the action in your fable. Write one story event on each line. Use only as many lines as you need. Draw arrows between events to show causes and effects that are connected. Finally, write how your fable will end.

Story events:

_____

_____

_____

_____

How my fable will end:

Now, use your notes to draft a fable that teaches a lesson.

Name _____ Date _____

"The Tiger Who Would Be King" by James Thurber
"The Ant and the Dove" by Leo Tolstoy
Support for Speaking and Listening: Oral Report

Use the following lines to take notes for your oral report on James Thurber or Leo Tolstoy.

Early life: _____

_____

_____

_____

How and why he became a writer: _____

_____

_____

_____

_____

Important published works: _____

_____

_____

_____

_____

Similarities and differences between this work and the author's other works:

_____

_____

_____

_____

_____

Name _____ Date _____

"**Arachne**" by Olivia E. Coolidge

Writing About the Big Question

How much do our communities shape us?

Big Question Vocabulary

belief	common	community	connection	culture
family	generation	group	history	influence
involve	isolate	participation	support	values

A. *Use one or more words from the list above to complete each sentence.*

1. Diana's grandmother said that her parents had told her animal stories with lessons, as a way to pass wisdom on from one _____ to the next.

2. Sanjay enjoys reading myths from the Hindu tradition and is happy that his _____ has a strong tradition of old stories.

3. Stories like "Jack and the Beanstalk" and *To Kill a Mockingbird* _____ the idea that it is good to fight evil, no matter how small you are.

4. Len's dad told interesting stories about the odd jobs he did to pay for college, as a way of passing on to his kids the _____ of education and hard work.

B. *Follow the directions in responding to each of the items below.*

1. List two different times when you learned a lesson from doing something wrong.

_____.

_____.

2. Write two sentences explaining one of the preceding experiences, and describe what you learned and how you felt about it. Use at least two of the Big Question vocabulary words.

_____

_____

C. *Complete the sentence below. Then, write a short paragraph in which you connect this experience to the Big Question.*

The story of _____ taught me that _____

_____

_____

_____

_____

_____

Name _____   Date _____

"**Arachne**" by Olivia E. Coolidge

Reading: Ask Questions to Analyze Cause-and-Effect Relationships

A **cause** is an event, an action, or a feeling that makes something happen. An **effect** is what happens. Sometimes, an effect can become the cause of another event. For example, seeing an empty soda can on the sidewalk can cause you to pick it up. The good example you set can then cause someone else to pick up litter when he or she sees it. As you read, look for clue words such as *because, as a result, therefore,* and *so* that signal cause-and-effect relationships. Then, **ask questions** such as "How did this happen?" and "What happened?" and "Why did this happen?" to help you follow the cause-and-effect relationships in a literary work.

DIRECTIONS: *Look at the organizer below. Some of the causes and effects and the questions you might ask about them in the first half of "Arachne" have been listed for you. Fill in the missing causes, questions, and effects. Notice as you work that events may follow each other without one causing the next. Also, notice that an effect can become the cause of another event.*

CAUSE   **EFFECT**

1. Arachne becomes famous as a weaver.	**2.** What happens as a result?	**3.** People say that Athene must have taught Arachne.

4. _____ _____	**5.** _____	**6.** _____ _____

7. _____ _____	**8.** What happens as a result?	**9.** The old woman shows herself to be Athene.

10. _____ _____	**11.** _____	**12.** Arachne competes with Athene.

Name _____ Date _____

"**Arachne**" by Olivia E. Coolidge
Literary Analysis: Myths

Myths are fictional tales that describe the actions of gods or heroes. Every culture has its own collection of myths. A myth can do one or more of the following:

- tell how the universe or a culture began
- explain something in nature, such as the return of spring after winter
- teach a lesson
- express a value, such as courage or honor

DIRECTIONS: *As you read "Arachne," look for examples of each characteristic of a myth. Use the examples to fill in the chart below. If you do not find an example of a particular characteristic, write "None" in the second column.*

A Myth Can . . .	How "Arachne" Shows This
1. Describe the actions of gods or heroes	
2. Tell how the universe or a culture began	
3. Explain something in nature	
4. Teach a lesson	
5. Express values and traditions that are important to the culture	

"**Arachne**" retold by Olivia E. Coolidge
Vocabulary Builder

Word List

humble   indignantly   mortal   obscure   obstinacy   strive

A. DIRECTIONS: *Complete each sentence below. Use examples or details from the story to show that you understand the meaning of the underlined vocabulary word. You may write additional sentences if necessary.*

Example: Some of Arachne's visitors were *nymphs*, _____.

Some of Arachne's visitors were nymphs, minor nature goddesses.

1. Arachne lived in an <u>obscure</u> village, a place that was _____

_____

2. Arachne showed her <u>obstinacy</u> when she _____

_____

3. Far from being <u>humble</u>, Arachne was actually _____

_____

4. The goddess spoke <u>indignantly</u>, because _____

_____

5. When we <u>strive</u> for a goal, we _____

_____

6. Someone who is <u>mortal</u> must eventually _____

_____

B. WORD STUDY: The Latin root *-mort-* means "death." Each of the following statements contains a word based on *-mort-*. Correct each statement to make it more logical.

1. His speed record seemed *immortal*, since it lasted about a week.

_____

2. The young woman was a *mortal*, and so she was equal to the mythological gods.

_____

"**Arachne**" retold by Olivia E. Coolidge
Conventions: Direct and Indirect Objects

Direct and Indirect Objects

Most sentences need words beyond a subject and a verb to complete their meaning. **Direct objects** and **indirect objects** complete ideas and make sentences more specific.

- A **direct object** is a noun or pronoun that receives the action of the verb and answers the question *Whom?* or *What?*
- They read their <u>stories</u> aloud. *What* was read aloud? their stories
  Stories receives the action of the verb *read*.
- The teacher greeted <u>them</u>. Greeted *whom?* them
  Them receives the action of the verb *greeted*.
- An **indirect object** is a noun or pronoun that names the person or thing to whom or for whom an action is done. An indirect object answers the question *To or for whom?* or *To or for what?*
- She sent <u>him</u> a poem. *To whom?* him *What?* a poem
  The indirect object is *him*.
  The direct object is *poem*.
- He wrote his <u>grandmother</u> and <u>grandfather</u> a limerick. *For whom?* grandmother and grandfather *What?* a limerick
  The compound indirect object is *grandmother* and *grandfather*.
  The direct object is *limerick*.

A. PRACTICE: *Underline the <u>direct object</u> once. Underline the <u>indirect object</u> twice. Then, write the question each object answers:* • What?   • To whom?   • For whom?

1. The new student gave the teacher his story.
   Direct object answers _____ Indirect object answers_____

2. The nurse offered Sally a cellphone.
   Direct object answers _____ Indirect object answers _____

3. Her mother sent the teacher a note about Sally's absence from school.
   Direct object answers _____ Indirect object answers _____

B. Writing Application: *Write four sentences about a shopping trip. Tell what you and an adult family member buy. Include a direct object and an indirect object in every sentence. Underline the direct objects once and the indirect objects twice. You may want to use some of these verbs:* bought, gave, showed, paid, sold, asked, found.

_____

_____

_____

Name _____ Date _____

Support for Writing to Sources: Comparison-and-Contrast Essay

Writing: "Arachne"

Use the following Venn diagram to take notes for your **comparison-and-contrast essay**. In the sections labeled "Arachne" and "Athene," take notes on ways that the two characters are different. In the middle section labeled "Both," take notes on ways that they are similar.

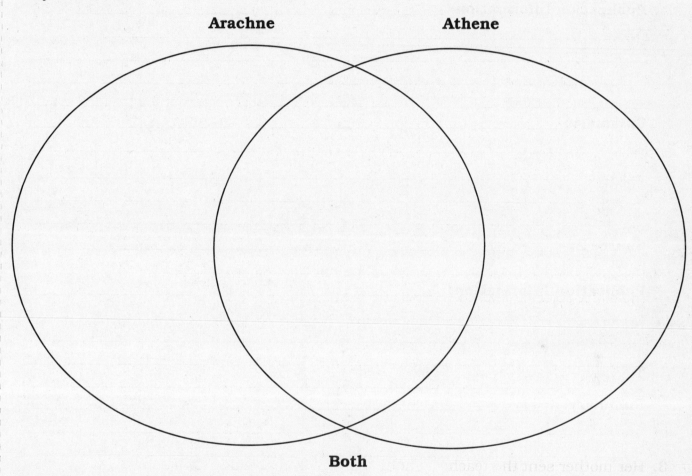

Arachne   **Athene**

Both

Now, use your notes to draft your essay.

"Arachne" retold by Olivia E. Coolidge

Support for Research and Technology: Annotated Bibliography

Use a library catalog or the Internet to find two reliable sources that provide information about the values and cultures of ancient Greece. Use this form to help you organize information for an **annotated bibliography.**

Source 1: _____

_____

Publication Information: _____

_____

_____

_____

Summary: _____

_____

_____

_____

_____

Source 2: _____

Publication Information: _____

_____

_____

_____

Summary: _____

_____

_____

_____

"**The Stone**" by Lloyd Alexander

Writing About the Big Question

How much do our communities shape us?

Big Question Vocabulary

belief	common	community	connection	culture
family	generation	group	history	influence
involve	isolate	participation	support	values

A. *Use one or more words from the list above to complete each sentence.*

1. Emilio's father wanted to move to a new town to shorten his commute, but he worried about the effect of the move on his wife and children, who had strong ties to the _____.

2. When Raina tried out for her school's sketch-comedy team, she didn't think about how her new activity would _____ her from her old friends.

3. When Josh wrote an offbeat, funny story for his class, he had no idea that his story would _____ his classmates to see him as a comic genius.

4. Dania finally saw a _____ between her reading and her choice of friends when she realized that she was drawn to people who reminded her of certain characters.

B. *Follow the directions in responding to each of the items below.*

1. List two different times when a goal of yours conflicted with what someone else wanted.

    _____.

    _____.

2. Write two sentences describing one of the preceding experiences. Tell whether you got your wish, what you learned, and how you felt about it. Use at least two of the Big Question vocabulary words.

    _____

    _____

C. *Complete the sentence below. Then, write a short paragraph in which you connect this experience to the Big Question.*

If I could make one wish come true for my life, I would want _____ because _____

_____

_____

_____.

"The Stone" by Lloyd Alexander
Reading: Setting a Purpose

Once you have **set your purpose for reading, adjust your reading rate** to help you accomplish that purpose. Adjust your reading rate by doing the following:

- When reading to remember information, make your reading rate slow and careful. Pause now and then to think about what you have read, and read difficult pages over again until you understand them. Also use a slow rate when reading descriptive passages with much detail.
- When reading for enjoyment, you may read more quickly. For example, read dialogue quickly to imitate the flow of a conversation.

DIRECTIONS: *As you read "The Stone," think about how you should adjust your reading rate for different sections of the folk tale. Complete the graphic organizer below by filling in passages that you read slowly, moderately, and quickly.*

Slowly	**Moderately**	**Quickly**
passage	passage	passage
passage	passage	passage

Name _____ Date _____

"The Stone" by Lloyd Alexander
Literary Analysis: Universal Theme

The theme of a literary work is its central idea or message about life or human nature. A **universal theme** is a message about life that is expressed regularly in many different cultures and time periods. Examples of universal themes include the importance of honesty, the power of love, and the danger of selfishness.

Look for a universal theme in a literary work by focusing on the story's main character, conflicts the character faces, changes he or she undergoes, and the effects of these changes. You can use a graphic organizer like the one shown to help you determine the universal theme.

DIRECTIONS: *Fill in the boxes with details from "The Stone." What universal theme do the details of the story lead to?*

Main Character

_____
_____

↓

Conflicts Character Faces

_____
_____
_____

↓

How Character Changes

_____
_____
_____

↓

Effects or Meaning of Change

_____
_____
_____

↓

Universal Theme

_____
_____
_____

"The Stone" by Lloyd Alexander
Vocabulary Builder

Word List

feeble   jubilation   plight   rue   sown   vanished

A. DIRECTIONS: *Write a **synonym** for each vocabulary word. Use a thesaurus if you need one. Write a sentence that includes the synonym. Be sure that your sentence makes the meaning of the word clear.*

Vocabulary word: heartening

Synonym: encouraging

Sentence: The sales rep found the good response to the product very encouraging.

1. Vocabulary word: **plight**   Synonym: _____

   Sentence: _____

2. Vocabulary word: **feeble**   Synonym: _____

   Sentence: _____

3. Vocabulary word: **sown**   Synonym: _____

   Sentence: _____

4. Vocabulary word: **vanished**   Synonym: _____

   Sentence: _____

5. Vocabulary word: **jubilation**   Synonym: _____

   Sentence: _____

6. Vocabulary word: **rue**   Synonym: _____

   Sentence: _____

B. WORD STUDY: The Latin root *-van-* means "empty." Answer each of the following questions using one of these words containing *-van-: vanish, evanescent, vain.*

1. What is a good way to make a rumor *vanish*?

   _____

2. Why would morning ground mist become *evanescent* as the day goes on?

   _____

3. How do you feel when your hard work has been in *vain*?

   _____

"The Stone" by Lloyd Alexander
Conventions: Independent and Dependent Clauses

A **clause** is a group of words with its own subject and verb. An **independent clause** has a subject and a verb and can stand on its own as a sentence. A **dependent clause** has a subject and a verb but cannot stand on its own as a complete sentence. A dependent clause may be introduced by a subordinating conjunction—such as *if, when, before,* or *because*—or a relative pronoun—such as *who, which,* or *that.*

Independent clause:	All winter we went to school.
Dependent clause:	**after** we returned home from school

A dependent clause depends on an independent clause to complete its meaning.

Dependent clause   **Independent clause**

All winter, after we returned home from school, we played in the snow.

A. PRACTICE: *Identify each of the following items as an independent or a dependent clause. Underline the word that introduces each dependent clause.*

Example: <u>when</u> the old man left his cottage   dependent

1. some people do not change _____

2. before you read a fable _____

3. she understood _____

4. that played a song _____

B. Writing Application: *Add to each dependent clause to make a complete sentence. Write the complete sentence on the line following each dependent clause.*

As we came to the end of the path,
As we came to the end of the path, we saw a cabin.

1. After he saw the old man,

_____.

2. Because he helped the dwarf,

_____.

3. Maibon, who finally got his wish, _____.

"The Stone" by Lloyd Alexander
Support for Writing to Sources: Plot Proposal

A plot proposal is a plan of story events. Use this page to take notes for your plot proposal that illustrates a universal theme.

Universal theme: _____

_____

Conflict or situation that could be used to demonstrate that theme: _____

_____

Events that lead to the theme:

_____

_____

_____

_____

_____

_____

_____

_____

_____

_____

_____

_____

_____

_____

_____

_____

_____

_____

_____

_____

Now use your notes to write your plot proposal.

Name _____ Date _____

"The Stone" by Lloyd Alexander
Support for Research and Technology:
Written and Visual Report

Use the lines below to take notes for your report on human aging. You may want to research some of the following topics, using the key words listed.

Gerontology (the study of aging) _____

_____

_____

_____

Geriatrics (branch of medicine related to old age) _____

_____

_____

_____

Aging _____

_____

_____

Aging Skin/Youthful Skin _____

_____

_____

Changes Caused by Aging _____

_____

_____

_____

Now, get together with your group to organize and outline the information you have gathered.

"Why the Tortoise's Shell Is Not Smooth" by Chinua Achebe
Writing About the Big Question

How much do our communities shape us?

Big Question Vocabulary

belief	common	community	connection	culture
family	generation	group	history	influence
involve	isolate	participation	support	values

A. *Use one or more words from the list above to complete each sentence.*

1. Rob plays funny tricks, but his tricks tend to _____ him a little because we don't trust him completely.

2. Because she had been on the wrong end of some practical jokes, Marina identified with stories that _____ the idea that playing tricks is wrong.

3. In a popular story, a _____ ignores a boy's genuine cries for help because he had tricked everyone before by crying "wolf" when there was no wolf.

4. Glenna learned the hard way that playing tricks, even harmless ones, could break an important _____ between her and her best friends.

B. *Follow the directions in responding to each of the items below.*

1. List two different times when someone played a trick on you.

_____.

_____.

2. Write two sentences explaining one of the preceding experiences, and describe what happened and how you felt about it. Use at least two of the Big Question vocabulary words.

_____

_____

C. *Complete the sentence below. Then, write a short paragraph in which you connect this experience to the Big Question.*

I played a trick on _____ when I _____

_____

_____

_____

_____

_____

"Why the Tortoise's Shell Is Not Smooth" by Chinua Achebe

Reading: Preview the Text to Set a Purpose for Reading

Your **purpose** for reading is the reason you read a text. Sometimes, you may choose a text based on a purpose you already have. Other times, you may set a purpose based on the kind of text you have in front of you. **Setting a purpose** helps you focus your reading. You might set a purpose to learn about a subject, to gain understanding, to take an action, or simply to read for enjoyment.

Preview the text before you begin to read. Look at the title, the pictures, and the beginnings of paragraphs to get an idea about the literary work. This will help you set a purpose or decide if the text will fit a purpose you already have.

DIRECTIONS: *Answer the following questions as you preview "Why the Tortoise's Shell Is Not Smooth." You can use questions like these as you preview any text.*

1. Look at the title. What ideas or feelings do you have about the title? _____
   _____

2. Who is the author? What do you know about this author? _____
   _____

3. Look at any photographs, drawings, or artwork in the text. How does the artwork help you set a purpose for reading? _____
   _____

4. Read the beginning of several paragraphs in the text. What kind of text does this seem to be? _____
   _____

5. Think about the clues you picked up during your preview. What purpose will you set to help you focus your reading of this text? _____
   _____

Name _____ Date _____

"Why the Tortoise's Shell Is Not Smooth" by Chinua Achebe
Literary Analysis: Personification

Personification is the representation of an animal or an object as if it had a human personality, intelligence, or emotions. In folk literature, personification is often used to give human qualities to animal characters. The actions of these animal characters can show human qualities, behavior, and problems in a humorous way.

DIRECTIONS: *As you read, think about the human and animal qualities shown by the tortoise, the birds, and the parrot in the story. Next to each name below, write two of that character's animal qualities on the lines at the left and two of that character's human qualities on the lines at the right. Treat the group of birds as one character.*

Animal Qualities   **Human Qualities**

_____   (1. Tortoise)   _____

_____   _____

_____   (2. the birds)   _____

_____   _____

_____   (3. Parrot)   _____

_____   _____

"Why the Tortoise's Shell Is Not Smooth" by Chinua Achebe
Vocabulary Builder

Word List

compound   cunning   custom   eloquent   famine   orator

A. DIRECTIONS: *Write your answer in a complete sentence using a Word List word.*

1. What might happen to people who live in a place where there is a *famine*?

   _____

2. What kind of job might require someone to be a skilled *orator*? Why?

   _____

3. Imagine that you have been asked to write an *eloquent* article for the paper. What will you write about?

   _____

4. Why is being *cunning* helpful in a competition?

   _____

5. How could a single house be turned into a *compound*?

   _____

6. What is your favorite family *custom*?

   _____

B. DIRECTIONS: *Choose the word or words that mean almost the same as the boldface vocabulary word. Write the letter for your answer choice on the line.*

____ 1. When Tortoise spoke at the party, his speech was **eloquent.**
   A. humorous   C. long
   B. expressive   D. illogical

____ 2. The rains ended the drought that had caused years of **famine.**
   A. food abundance   C. food shortage
   B. flooding   D. rebellion

____ 3. A child whose mother is a famous storyteller might want to be a great **orator.**
   A. doctor   C. writer
   B. leader   D. speaker

C. WORD STUDY: The suffix *-ary* means "related to or connected with." Change each of the italicized words in parentheses to a word that ends in *-ary.*

1. It is a *(custom)* _____ practice in many societies to celebrate an adolescent's passage to manhood or womanhood.

2. A sensitive child might have an *(imagine)* _____ friend.

3. My mother was given the *(honor)* _____ title of professor emeritus.

Name _____ Date _____

Conventions: Sentences—Simple, Compound, and Complex Sentence Structure

Sentences can be classified according to the number and kinds of their **clauses**—groups of words with their own subjects and verbs.

- A **simple sentence** has one independent clause.

  The sun came out. Sam and Al raced. Priya stayed inside and played.

- A **compound sentence** has two or more independent clauses. Independent clauses are usually joined by a comma and a conjunction such as *and, but, or, nor,* or *yet.*

  We packed our bags, Mom made lunch, <u>and</u> Dad put gas in the car.

- A **complex sentence** has one independent clause and one or more dependent clauses. Words that begin dependent clauses may be subordinating conjunctions— such as *after, because, before, if,* and *when*—or relative pronouns—such as, *which, that, who,* and *whom.*

  I have a cousin <u>who</u> is a performer.

A. PRACTICE: *Identify each sentence below. Write* **S** *if it is a simple sentence,* **CP** *if it is a compound sentence, or* **CX** *if it is a complex sentence.*

____ 1. Nobody knows who first made up myths and folk tales.

____ 2. Myths, folk tales, and fables are usually stories from oral tradition.

____ 3. In some myths, when humans are too proud, they are punished by the gods.

____ 4. Good behavior is rewarded, and bad behavior has serious consequences.

B. Writing Application: *Imagine that you are at an amusement park with friends. Write a paragraph about the things you might see and do there. Use at least one of each type of sentence in your paragraph.*

_____

_____

_____

_____

_____

_____

_____

_____

_____

"Why the Tortoise's Shell Is Not Smooth" by Chinua Achebe

Support for Writing to Sources: Invitation

Use the graphic organizer below to record details for an invitation to the feast in the sky. Review the story to find details you can use. Begin your invitation with a paragraph that describes the purpose of the gathering. Make up additional details, such as time and date, that are not provided in the story. In the empty space below, you may want to add artwork that you can copy when you create your invitation.

Come to _____

Purpose: _____

_____

_____

_____

Place: _____

Date: _____

Time: _____

Add artwork below if you want to. Then, create your invitation.

Name _____ Date _____

"Why the Tortoise's Shell Is Not Smooth" by Chinua Achebe
Support for Speaking and Listening: Dramatic Reading

To prepare for your dramatic reading, list the person in your group who will read each part. If possible, ask your teacher to make copies of the text so each student can mark up his or her own copy to show who will say which words and how the words should be said. You may want to have three group members read together as the birds.

Ekwefi the storyteller (reads the parts that are not dialogue): _____

The Birds: _____

Tortoise: _____

Answer the following questions about the part you will be reading.

What are the most important lines I have? _____
_____
_____
_____

How should I say them? _____
_____
_____

Which words should I stress for effect? _____
_____
_____

What gestures can I use for effect? _____
_____
_____

"**Mowgli's Brothers**" by Rudyard Kipling
from **James and the Giant Peach** by Roald Dahl
Writing About the Big Question

THE BIG ?

How much do our communities shape us?

Big Question Vocabulary

belief	common	community	connection	culture
family	generation	group	history	influence
involve	isolate	participation	support	values

A. *Use one or more words from the list above to complete each sentence.*

1. When his family moved to the United States from India, Siddhartha was a little nervous about living in a place with such a different _____ from his own, but he settled in very quickly.

2. LeeAnn loved watching the life going on in her ant farm, in which individuals worked together for the _____ good.

3. Jen's favorite fantasy is to time-travel to a different period in _____. Her favorite time-travel destination would be Elizabethan England, where she could meet William Shakespeare.

4. Jaime is fascinated with the social behavior of wolves, especially the way they recognize different levels of status within their _____.

B. *Follow the directions in responding to each of the items below.*

1. List two different times when you were in a very unusual environment.

_____.

_____.

2. Write two sentences describing one of the preceding experiences. Tell what it was like and how you felt about it. Use at least two of the Big Question vocabulary words.

_____

_____

C. *Complete the sentence below. Then, write a short paragraph in which you connect this experience to the Big Question.*

If I could spend time in any other place in the universe, I would like to go to _____ because _____

_____

_____

"Mowgli's Brothers" by Rudyard Kipling
from James and the Giant Peach by Roald Dahl
Literary Analysis: Elements of Fantasy

Fantasy is imaginative writing that contains elements not found in real life. Stories about talking animals, books that come to life, or time travel are all examples of fantasy. Many fantastic stories, however, contain **realistic elements**—characters, events, or situations that are true to life. In a fantastic story about a talking cat, for example, the cat might do many things that real cats do. She might purr, stretch, and flex her claws, all of which are real-life cat behaviors.

DIRECTIONS: *Read each passage below and answer the questions.*

from "Mowgli's Brothers" by Rudyard Kipling

It was the jackal—Tabaqui the Dishlicker—and the wolves of India despise Tabaqui because he runs about making mischief, and telling tales, and eating rags and pieces of leather from the village rubbish-heaps. . . .

"Enter, then, and look," said Father Wolf, stiffly, "but there is no food here."

"For a wolf, no," said Tabaqui, "but for so mean a person as myself a dry bone is a good feast. Who are we, the Gidur-log [the jackal-people], to pick and choose?" He scuttled to the back of the cave, where he found the bone of a buck with some meat on it, and sat cracking the end merrily.

1. List two details that are not found in real life.

   _____

2. List two details that are true to life.

   _____

from James and the Giant Peach by Roald Dahl

"Is that a Glow-worm?" asked James, staring at the light. "It doesn't look like a worm of any sort to me."

"Of course it's a Glow-worm," the Centipede answered. "At least that's what she calls herself. Although actually you are quite right. She isn't really a worm at all. Glow-worms are never worms. They are simply lady fireflies without wings. Wake up, you lazy beast!"

But the Glow-worm didn't stir, so the Centipede reached out of his hammock and picked up one of his boots from the floor. "Put out that wretched light!" he shouted, hurling the boot up at the ceiling.

3. List two details that are not found in real life.

   _____

4. List two details that are true to life.

   _____

"Mowgli's Brothers" by Rudyard Kipling
from **James and the Giant Peach** by Roald Dahl
Vocabulary Builder

Word List

colossal   dispute   fostering   intently   monotonous   quarry

A. DIRECTIONS: *Each sentence below features a word from the Word List. If the sentence makes sense, explain why. If it does not make sense, write a new sentence using the word correctly.*

1. I watched the *colossal* specks of dust drift through the ray of sun.

   _____

2. "Please stop *fostering* me!" Ella said to her little brother.

   _____

3. We ended our *dispute* by shaking hands and agreeing to disagree.

   _____

4. If you read the book *intently*, you will probably miss some important details.

   _____

5. The leopard eyed his *quarry* from a low tree branch and prepared to pounce.

   _____

6. True, the adventure movie was long, but it was also exciting and *monotonous*!

   _____

B. DIRECTIONS: *Use a word from the Word List to complete each analogy. Your choice should create a word pair whose relationship matches the relationship between the first two words given.*

1. *Run* is to *quickly* as *work* is to _____.
2. *Elf* is to *small* as *giant* is to _____.
3. *Idea* is to *thought* as *disagreement* is to _____.
4. *Detective* is to *clue* as *hunter* is to _____.

"Mowgli's Brothers" by Rudyard Kipling

from **James and the Giant Peach** by Roald Dahl

Writing to Compare Elements of Fantasy

Before you draft your essay comparing and contrasting each story's fantastic and realistic elements, complete the graphic organizers below. For each graphic organizer, decide which story best fits each sentence.

Animals

The animals in _____ seem more realistic because _____

_____.

In contrast, the animals in _____ do more fantastic things such as

_____.

Human Character

The boy in _____ is more fantastic because he _____

_____.

In contrast, the boy in _____ does more realistic things such as ___

_____.

Setting

The setting in _____ seems more realistic because _____

_____.

In contrast, the setting in _____ seems more fantastic because ____

_____.

Situation

The situation in _____ *might* really happen because _____

_____.

In contrast, the situation in _____ could never happen because ____

_____.

Now, use your notes to write an essay comparing and contrasting the authors' use of fantastic and realistic elements in these two stories. Begin your essay by stating which story contains more fantastic elements overall.

Cause-and-Effect Essay

Prewriting: Narrowing Your Topic

Use this topic web to help you evaluate and narrow your topic. Write your topic in the leftmost circle. Then, write connected ideas inside the upper half of the four connected circles. Finally, write additional ideas related to each subtopic in the lower half of the circles.

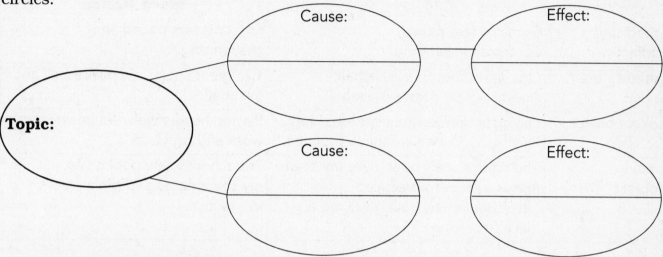

Drafting: Organizing Details

Select one of the following graphic organizers and list the details of your essay. Use this organizational pattern as you draft your essay.

Many Causes/Single Effect

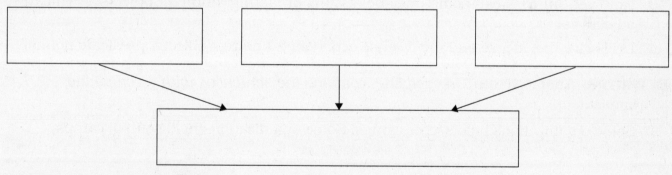

Single Cause/Many Effects

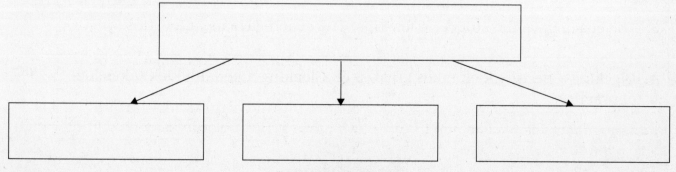

Writer's Toolbox
Sentence Fluency: Revising Choppy Sentences

The chart shows how combining subject complements and direct and indirect objects eliminates choppy sentences.

Complement	Choppy Sentences	Revised Sentences That Sound Much Better
predicate adjective	Soccer is **fast-paced**. Soccer is **challenging**.	Soccer is **fast-paced** and **challenging**.
predicate noun	One great sport is **basketball**. Another great sport is **baseball**.	Two great sports are **basketball** and **baseball**.
direct object	Playing hockey well requires hard **work**. Playing hockey well requires **practice**.	Playing hockey well requires hard **work** and **practice**.
indirect object	The school's new pool gives **my team-mates** a place to practice. The school's new pool gives **me** a place to practice.	The school's new pool gives **my teammates** and **me** a place to practice.

A. PRACTICE: *Circle the subject complements and direct and indirect objects in each sentence. Then, underline their type in parentheses.*

1. Football is a sport and also entertainment. (indirect objects, predicate nouns)

2. Players wear helmets and pads for protection. (direct objects, predicate nouns)

3. However, injuries can sometimes be serious or lasting. (indirect objects, predicate adjectives)

4. Drills give the offense and the defense experience. (indirect objects, predicate nouns)

B. WRITING APPLICATION: *On each line, combine the sentences with a compound complement.*

1. Some organizations hold soccer camps. Some organizations hold softball camps.

_____

2. Players must be strong. Players must be fit.

_____

3. The coach gave the stopper a few tips. The coach gave me a few tips.

_____

4. Blocking a penalty kick takes great skill. Blocking a penalty kick takes lots of practice.

_____

Prologue from **"The Whale Rider"** by Witi Ihimaera
Vocabulary Builder

Selection Vocabulary

apex   teemed   yearning

A. DIRECTIONS: *Look at the italicized word in each sentence. Then, for each sentence, explain whether it makes sense. If it does not make sense, write a new sentence using the word correctly.*

1. After many years' experience, she became president, reaching the *apex* of her career.

   _____

2. The large tank containing just two little goldfish *teemed* with fish.

   _____

3. *Yearning* for another bone, the dog stood by the table, its tail wagging,

   _____

Academic Vocabulary

observe   sensory   reveal

B. DIRECTIONS: *Create two different sentences for each of the following words. Try to use the word to explain something entirely different in your second sentence.*

> **Example:** The committee leader wanted to <u>chair</u> the meeting.
> The teacher laid a pencil on top of every <u>chair</u>.

OBSERVE

1. _____

2. _____

SENSORY

3. _____

4. _____

REVEAL

5. _____

6. _____

Prologue from "**The Whale Rider**" by Witi Ihimaera
Take Notes for Discussion

Before the Partner Discussion: Read the passage from the selection in your textbook that begins and ends as shown below.

> The sun rose and set, rose and set … trembled from the impact of that downward plunging.

During the Discussion: As you and your partner discuss each question, take notes on how your partner's ideas either differ from or build upon your own.

Discussion Questions	Other Responses	Comparison to My Responses
1. What characteristics of whales might inspire people to develop myths about them?		
2. Would this passage have the same impact if a different type of creature had appeared in the sea? Why or why not?		

Prologue from **"The Whale Rider"** by Witi Ihimaera
Take Notes for Writing to Sources

Planning Your Informative Text: Before you begin drafting your **cause-and-effect essay,** use the chart below to organize your ideas.

---

1. Details that describe the land and sea at different points in the story:

_____

_____

_____

_____

_____

_____

_____

_____

2. Details that show cause-and-effect relationships:

_____

_____

_____

_____

_____

_____

_____

_____

3. Transitional words and phrases that will clarify the cause-and-effect relationships:

_____

_____

_____

_____

_____

Name _____ Date _____

Prologue from **"The Whale Rider"** by Witi Ihimaera
Take Notes for Research

As you research **the role of myths in society and what myths from different cultures have in common,** use the forms below to take notes from your sources. As necessary, continue your notes on the back of this page, on note cards, or in a word-processing document.

Myths in Society	
Main Idea _____ _____	Main Idea _____ _____
Quotation or Paraphrase _____ _____ _____ _____	Quotation or Paraphrase _____ _____ _____ _____
Source Information _____ _____ _____ _____	Source Information _____ _____ _____ _____
Main Idea _____ _____	Main Idea _____ _____
Quotation or Paraphrase _____ _____ _____ _____	Quotation or Paraphrase _____ _____ _____ _____
Source Information _____ _____ _____ _____	Source Information _____ _____ _____ _____

"The Case of the Monkeys That Fell From the Trees" by Susan E. Quinlan
Vocabulary Builder

Selection Vocabulary

abruptly   distress   incidents

A. DIRECTIONS: *Write the letter of the word or phrase that is closest in meaning to the vocabulary word.*

_____ 1. **ABRUPTLY**

      A. suddenly   C. slowly

      B. soon   D. amazingly

_____ 2. **DISTRESS**

      A. anger   C. disease

      B. pain or discomfort   D. disgust

_____ 3. **INCIDENTS**

      A. events   C. accidents

      B. remembrances   D. riots

Academic Vocabulary

investigate   observation   study

B. DIRECTIONS: *Write a response to each question. Make sure to use the italicized word at least once in your response.*

1. Why might it be useful to *investigate* the ingredients of a certain food? Explain.

_____

_____

2. How does making an *observation* of monkeys help you understand them? Explain.

_____

_____

3. What is an important part of a *study* of animal behavior? Explain.

_____

_____

"The Case of the Monkeys That Fell From the Trees" by Susan E. Quinlan
Take Notes for Discussion

Before the Panel Discussion: Read the following passage from the selection.

Glander and other researchers have gathered some evidence that howlers and other monkeys sometimes select poisonous leaves for medicinal purposes, such as ridding themselves of parasites. Glander thinks scientists searching for new medicines for people might get some useful tips from howlers.

During the Discussion: As the panel discusses each question, take notes on how other students' ideas either differ from or build upon your own.

Discussion Questions	Other Ideas Expressed	Comparison to My Own Ideas
1. How might information learned through scientific research lead Glander and others to new research questions?	_____ _____ _____ _____ _____ _____ _____ _____ _____ _____	_____ _____ _____ _____ _____ _____ _____ _____ _____ _____
2. What does the passage reveal about a way in which howlers are like people?	_____ _____ _____ _____ _____ _____ _____ _____ _____ _____ _____	_____ _____ _____ _____ _____ _____ _____ _____ _____ _____ _____

Name _____ Date _____

"The Case of the Monkeys That Fell From the Trees" by Susan E. Quinlan
Take Notes for Research

As you research **more about the scientific method and how and when it was developed,** use the chart below to take notes from your sources. As necessary, continue your notes on the back of this page, on note cards, or in a word-processing document.

Source Information   Check one: ☐ Primary Source   ☐ Secondary Source

Title: _____   Author: _____

Publication Information: _____

Page(s): _____

Main Idea: _____

_____

Quotation or Paraphrase: _____

_____

Source Information   Check one: ☐ Primary Source   ☐ Secondary Source

Title: _____   Author: _____

Publication Information: _____

Page(s): _____

Main Idea: _____

_____

Quotation or Paraphrase: _____

_____

Source Information   Check one: ☐ Primary Source   ☐ Secondary Source

Title: _____   Author: _____

Publication Information: _____

Page(s): _____

Main Idea: _____

_____

Quotation or Paraphrase: _____

_____

Name _____ Date _____

"The Case of the Monkeys That Fell From the Trees" by Susan E. Quinlan
Take Notes for Writing to Sources

Planning Your Informative Text: Before you begin drafting your **explanation,** use the chart below to organize your ideas.

1. Notes about your introduction to the Glanders' question and their methods:

_____
_____
_____

2. Relevant facts and concrete details from the article:

_____
_____
_____
_____
_____
_____
_____

3. Order of steps followed by the Glanders:

_____
_____
_____
_____
_____
_____
_____
_____
_____
_____

4. Notes for your conclusion:

_____
_____
_____
_____

Name _____ Date _____

"Rescuers to Carry Oxygen Masks for Pets" by Associated Press
Vocabulary Builder

Selection Vocabulary

inhalation   resuscitation   unsolicited

A. DIRECTIONS: *Fill in the blank in each sentence with the correct vocabulary word. Then write your own sentence using that vocabulary word.*

1. He had stopped breathing, so we had to attempt _____.

_____

2. Our help was _____, but we gave it anyway.

_____

3. The man had suffered from smoke _____.

_____

Academic Vocabulary

authorities   quotation   support

B. DIRECTIONS: *Write one example of people or things that demonstrate the meaning of each word. Follow this example.*

RUDIMENTS: the steps in boiling an egg

1. AUTHORITIES: _____

2. QUOTATION: _____

3. SUPPORT: _____

Name _____ Date _____

"Rescuers to Carry Oxygen Masks for Pets" by Associated Press
Take Notes for Discussion

Before the Partner Discussion: Read the following passage from the selection.

> "What we've done so far is use the masks as a way to remind people to get out of their residence in the event of a fire and don't go searching for pets," she said. "Firefighters will care for any pets we find in the event they suffer from smoke inhalation."

During the Discussion: As you and your partner discuss each question, take notes on how your partner's ideas either differ from or build upon your own.

Discussion Questions	Other Ideas Expressed	Comparison to My Own Ideas
1. What did the Madison Fire Department hope would happen after it provided pet oxygen masks to firefighters?		
2. How might use of the masks help accomplish this goal?		

Name _____ Date _____

As you research **why people and animals may need oxygen after being exposed to a fire and why pets need specialized oxygen masks,** you can use the forms below. As necessary, continue your notes on the back of this page, on note cards, or in a word-processing document.

Source Information   Check one: ☐ Primary Source   ☐ Secondary Source

Title: _____   Author: _____

Publication Information: _____

Page(s): _____

Main Idea: _____

_____

Quotation or Paraphrase: _____

_____

Source Information   Check one: ☐ Primary Source   ☐ Secondary Source

Title: _____   Author: _____

Publication Information: _____

Page(s): _____

Main Idea: _____

_____

Quotation or Paraphrase: _____

_____

Source Information   Check one: ☐ Primary Source   ☐ Secondary Source

Title: _____   Author: _____

Publication Information: _____

Page(s): _____

Main Idea: _____

_____

Quotation or Paraphrase: _____

_____

"Rescuers to Carry Oxygen Masks for Pets" by Associated Press
Take Notes for Writing to Sources

Planning Your Narrative: Before you begin drafting your **nonfiction narrative,** use the chart below to organize your ideas.

1. Notes for your introduction that will include evidence from the article:

_____

_____

_____

2. Vivid words that will describe the pet and the situation:

_____

_____

_____

_____

_____

_____

_____

3. Steps that ensured the pet's safety:

_____

_____

_____

_____

_____

_____

_____

_____

4. Notes for your conclusion:

_____

_____

_____

_____

Name _____ Date _____

Infographic: Pet Ownership 2012 Statistics
Vocabulary Builder and Take Notes for Discussion

Academic Vocabulary

explain   generalization   subject

DIRECTIONS: *Write two different sentences for each of the following words. Try to use the word to explain something entirely different in your second sentence.*

Example: At the talent show, Gloria sang with great <u>feeling</u>.
I have a <u>feeling</u> that we are being watched.

1. **EXPLAIN** _____

_____

2. **GENERALIZATION** _____

_____

3. **SUBJECT** _____

_____

Take Notes for Discussion

During the Class Discussion: As you discuss each question, take notes on how other students' ideas either differ from or build upon your own.

Discussion Questions	Other Ideas Expressed	Comparison to My Own Ideas
1. Why might kennel boarding be more of an expense for dog owners than for cat owners?		
2. How can you explain the large difference between the number of people who own freshwater fish and saltwater fish?		

"The Old Woman Who Lived With the Wolves" by Chief Luther Standing Bear
Vocabulary Builder

Selection Vocabulary

coaxed   mystified   traversed

A. DIRECTIONS: *On the line before the sentence, write* T *if the statement is true or* F *if the statement is false. Then, explain your answer.*

_____ 1. Someone who *traversed* a frozen pond would have walked around the pond.

   _____

_____ 2. A child who is frightened may have to be *coaxed* to come out of hiding.

   _____

_____ 3. Someone who saw a person disappear might be *mystified*.

   _____

Academic Vocabulary

indicate   resolve   sensory

B. DIRECTIONS: *Complete each sentence with a word, phrase, or clause that contains a context clue for the italicized word.*

1. The facts seem to *indicate* that the dog is lost, so we _____

   _____

2. I hope Anna will *resolve* to finish the race, because _____

   _____

3. The *sensory* details in the story helped me _____

   _____

Name _____ Date _____

"The Old Woman Who Lived With the Wolves" by Chief Luther Standing Bear
Take Notes for Discussion

Before the Group Discussion: Read the passage from the selection in your textbook that begins and ends as shown below.

The blizzard ranged outside … toward the camp of her people.

During the Discussion: As your group discusses each question, take notes on how other students' ideas either differ from or build upon your own.

Discussion Questions	Other Ideas Expressed	Comparison to My Own Ideas
1. What does Marpiyawin learn from living with the wolves?		
2. How are the communities of the wolves and the Sioux alike?		

Name _____ Date _____

Take Notes for Research

As you research **when and how people domesticated, or tamed, dogs, sheep, cows, and horses and how both humans and animals benefited,** you can use the organizer below to take notes from your sources. As necessary, continue your notes on the back of this page, on note cards, or in a word-processing document.

Domestication of Animals	
Main Idea _____ _____ Quotation or Paraphrase _____ _____ _____ _____ _____ Source Information _____ _____ _____ _____	Main Idea _____ _____ Quotation or Paraphrase _____ _____ _____ _____ _____ Source Information _____ _____ _____ _____
Main Idea _____ _____ Quotation or Paraphrase _____ _____ _____ _____ _____ Source Information _____ _____ _____ _____	Main Idea _____ _____ Quotation or Paraphrase _____ _____ _____ _____ _____ Source Information _____ _____ _____ _____

Name _____ Date _____

"The Old Woman Who Lived With the Wolves" by Chief Luther Standing Bear
Take Notes for Writing to Sources

Planning Your Informative Essay: Before you begin drafting your **informative essay,** use the chart below to organize your ideas.

1. Notes for your introduction, including reasons that support your claim:

_____

_____

_____

_____

_____

_____

2. Details and examples from the story:

_____

_____

_____

_____

_____

_____

_____

_____

_____

_____

3. Transition words that will clarify the relationships between your claim and supporting details:

_____

_____

_____

_____

_____

_____

_____

"Satellites and Sea Lions: Working Together to Improve Ocean Models"
NASA News Release
Vocabulary Builder

Selection Vocabulary

marine   meteorologists   navigate

A. DIRECTIONS: *Write one example of people or things that demonstrate the meaning of each word. Follow this example.*

INGREDIENTS: a list of items for cooking or baking a recipe

1. **MARINE:** _____

_____

2. **METEOROLOGISTS:**

_____

3. **NAVIGATE:** _____

_____

Academic Vocabulary

collaboratively   credible   interaction

B. DIRECTIONS: *Revise each sentence so that the italicized vocabulary word is used logically. Be sure not to change the vocabulary word.*

1. We were asked to work *collaboratively*, so we each went our separate ways.

_____

2. We knew the information was not *credible*, so we were satisfied that we had found out the truth.

_____

3. The *interaction* between the two groups may cause some trouble, since the groups get along well.

_____

Name _____ Date _____

"Satellites and Sea Lions: Working Together to Improve Ocean Models"
NASA News Release
Take Notes for Discussion

Before the Class Discussion: Read the passage from the selection in your textbook that begins and ends as shown below.

> What is most important about using marine animals ... what is going to happen to habitats of marine animals."

During the Discussion: As the class discusses each question, take notes on how other students' ideas either differ from or build upon your own.

Discussion Questions	Other Ideas Expressed	Comparison to My Own Ideas
1. How does sharing information lead people to a better understanding of animals?		
2. What information about climate can the researchers learn from animals?		

Name _____ Date _____

"Satellites and Sea Lions: Working Together to Improve Ocean Models"
NASA News Release
Take Notes for Research

As you research **different types of scientists who study the ocean and its creatures,** you can use the organizer below to take notes from your sources. As necessary, continue your notes on the back of this page, on note cards, or in a word-processing document.

Scientists Who Study the Ocean

Main Idea _____

_____

Quotation or Paraphrase _____

_____

_____

_____

_____

Source Information _____

_____

_____

_____

_____

Main Idea _____

_____

Quotation or Paraphrase _____

_____

_____

_____

_____

Source Information _____

_____

_____

_____

_____

Main Idea _____

_____

Quotation or Paraphrase _____

_____

_____

_____

_____

Source Information _____

_____

_____

_____

Main Idea _____

_____

Quotation or Paraphrase _____

_____

_____

_____

_____

Source Information _____

_____

_____

_____

Name _____ Date _____

Take Notes for Writing to Sources

Planning Your Argument: Before you begin drafting your **persuasive letter,** use the chart below to organize your ideas.

1. Notes for presentation of your claim:

_____

_____

_____

2. Opposing position and your refutation:

_____

_____

_____

_____

_____

_____

_____

3. Reasons and evidence from the text that support your claim:

_____

_____

_____

_____

_____

_____

4. Transitional words and phrases that will clarify the relationships among the reasons and evidence that support your claim:

_____

_____

_____

5. Notes for your conclusion:

_____

_____

_____

Name _____ Date _____

"**Turkeys**" by Bailey White
Vocabulary Builder

Selection Vocabulary

demise   dilution   vigilance

A. DIRECTIONS: *Circle the letter of the word or phrase that is closest in meaning to each word in capital letters.*

1. VIGILANCE:

   A. attack   C. watchfulness

   B. nonsense   D. guardianship

2. DILUTION:

   A. enlarge   C. intelligence

   B. sensitive   D. process of weakening

3. DEMISE:

   A. beginning   C. health

   B. death   D. sickness

Academic Vocabulary

crucial

B. DIRECTIONS: *Follow the directions for each item.*

1. *Complete the following sentence with a word, phrase, or clause that contains a context clue for the italicized word.*

   Getting to the meeting on time is *crucial*, because _____

   _____

2. *Revise the following sentence so that the italicized vocabulary word is used logically. Do not change the vocabulary word.*

   The lawyer found *crucial* evidence that was not important to her case.

   _____

3. *Write a sentence about a crucial decision that the president must make. Use the word* crucial *in the sentence.*

   _____

All-in-One Workbook
© Pearson Education, Inc. All rights reserved.
290

Name _____ Date _____

"Turkeys" by Bailey White
Take Notes for Discussion

Before the Class Discussion: Read the passage from the selection in your textbook that begins and ends as shown below.

> Finally, in late summer, the day came ... "One hundred percent pure wild turkey!" they said.

During the Discussion: As the class discusses each question, take notes on how other students' ideas either differ from or build upon your own.

Discussion Questions	Other Ideas Expressed	Comparison to My Own Ideas
1. How is the behavior of the humans and turkeys related?	_____ _____ _____ _____ _____ _____ _____ _____ _____ _____	_____ _____ _____ _____ _____ _____ _____ _____ _____ _____
2. What idea about humans and animals is revealed in this passage?	_____ _____ _____ _____ _____ _____ _____ _____ _____ _____	_____ _____ _____ _____ _____ _____ _____ _____ _____ _____

Name _____ Date _____

Take Notes for Research

As you research **wild turkeys and how people helped them make a comeback,** use the forms below to take notes from your sources. As necessary, continue your notes on the back of this page, on note cards, or in a word-processing document.

Source Information   Check one: ☐ Primary Source   ☐ Secondary Source

Title: _____   Author: _____

Publication Information: _____

Page(s): _____

Main Idea: _____

_____

Quotation or Paraphrase: _____

_____

Source Information   Check one: ☐ Primary Source   ☐ Secondary Source

Title: _____   Author: _____

Publication Information: _____

Page(s): _____

Main Idea: _____

_____

Quotation or Paraphrase: _____

_____

Source Information   Check one: ☐ Primary Source   ☐ Secondary Source

Title: _____   Author: _____

Publication Information: _____

Page(s): _____

Main Idea: _____

_____

Quotation or Paraphrase: _____

_____

"Turkeys" by Bailey White
Take Notes for Writing to Sources

Planning Your Argument: Before you begin drafting your **persuasive essay,** use the chart below to organize your ideas.

1. Notes for the introduction to your claim:

_____

_____

_____

_____

2. Logical reasoning and information from the text that will support your claim:

_____

_____

_____

_____

_____

_____

_____

_____

_____

_____

_____

3. Transition words, phrases, and clauses that will connect your claim and reasons:

_____

_____

_____

_____

4. Notes for your strong concluding statement:

_____

_____

_____

_____